Therapist as Life Coach
Transforming Your Practice

Therapist as Life Coach
Transforming Your Practice

Patrick Williams

Deborah C. Davis

W. W. Norton & Company
New York • London

For information about permission to reproduce selections from this book, write to
Permissions, W. W. Norton & Company, Inc., 500 Fifth Avenue, New York, NY 10110

The text of this book is composed in Garamond
with the display set in Officina Sans
Book design and composition by Paradigm Graphics
Manufacturing by The Haddon Craftsmen, Inc.
Production Manager: Anna Oler

Library of Congress Cataloging-in-Publication Data

Williams, Patrick, 1950-
    Therapist as life coach : transforming your practice / Patrick
Williams, Deborah C. Davis.
        p. cm.
"A Norton professional book."
Includes bibliographical references and index.
ISBN 0-393-70341-X
    1. Counseling. 2. Conduct of life. I. Davis, Deborah C. II. Title.

BF637.C6.W54 2002
158'.3--dc21   2002016641

W. W. Norton & Company, Inc.
500 Fifth Avenue, New York, NY 10110
www.wwnorton.com

W. W. Norton & Company Ltd.
Castle House, 75/76 Wells Street, London W1T 3QT

1 2 3 4 5 6 7 8 9 0

To Vernon Williams and Raymond D. Davis

Contents

Acknowledgments

Many people have influenced our book. We recognize, after working for years in the helping profession as practitioners and teachers, that the fabric of who we are and what we say today is a composite of the many people who have touched us along the way. We've learned from clients, teachers, counselors, coaches, and a myriad of other wise individuals. We thank all of them for their wonderful contributions to our lives.

Throughout our book we've made a good faith effort to give credit to those who originally created the information we share. Some of the quotes we have included are part of collections we've maintained for years. We hope that you enjoy them as we did, and that we've truly given all recognition where it is due.

There are some individuals we especially want to acknowledge for their contributions to the coaching profession and this particular book. To Dave Ellis, Laura Berman Fortgang, Frederic Hudson, Thomas Leonard, Sherry Lowry, Diane Menendez, Julio Olalla, Cheryl Richardson, Sandy Vilas, and Laura Whitworth, we offer our deepest respect and appreciation for their support and their pioneering spirit in creating the profession of life coaching.

We also thank Deborah Malmud, Director of Norton Professional Books, for her belief in our message to life coaches, her faith in our abilities to deliver the product, and her dedication to see that our book achieved the professional level we desired.

This book literally would not be in your hands but for the tireless dedication of Edwina Adams who prepared our manuscript word by word. She graciously accepted our various forms of writing and helped us find one voice through which to speak our message. It was her dedication and encouragement that helped our dream materialize, and we will be forever grateful.

Finally, we dedicate this book to our fathers, Vernon Williams and Raymond D. Davis. These men were our first life coaches, and through their words and deeds we learned to be friendly, open minded, and willing to laugh at ourselves. They taught us to give whatever we took on in life our full attention and best work. We believe they would have enjoyed our book. We hope you do too.

Introduction

How different our lives are when we really know what is deeply important to us, and, keeping that picture in mind, we manage ourselves each day to be and do what really matters most.

—Stephen R. Covey

The experience of reading this book, like many life coaching sessions, is eye-opening. It demonstrates what is possible when humans dream, communicate, and strive to achieve that which seemed only a faint and distant goal in the quiet corners of their minds.

We presented our first joint workshop in October 1998 at a conference of the American Association of Marriage and Family Therapists. We didn't know what to expect for participation even though we sensed there was some interest in life coaching. To our delight, over 75 family therapists filled the room for our presentation and eagerly participated in the discussion. Participants' stories revolved around the theme of wanting something "more" out of their helping relationships. They described feeling tired, frustrated, discouraged, and unable to "make a difference" in individual lives the way they once believed possible. We understood clearly what they were saying as we too had shared similar feelings and frustrations.

Before we go any further, we'd like to tell you a little bit about our backgrounds and how we came together on this book.

In the 1970s Pat obtained degrees in humanistic psychology and transpersonal psychology, which, even then, were not typical psychologist studies. However, he did become a psychologist and actually had fun until managed care came along. Before he even realized what had happened, his clients and how he did business changed. At first he didn't even realize what was happening, but suddenly, it dawned on him that he wasn't working with people who wanted to improve their lives any more, he was working with people who had one serious mental illness after another. After doing some executive coaching for a while to infuse new energy into his practice, he jumped "feet first" into coaching. He hired a coach, trained at Coach University,* and found quickly that his heart and soul were in the right place. He subsequently closed his psychology practice and went full time into coaching and training therapists interested in becoming coaches.

Deb came to life coaching after being a counselor and family therapist. She spent most of her career as a college counselor, and she taught in a graduate counselor education program. Deb was commended as an exemplary teacher and great mentor for adult learners. In 1994 she noticed the term "coaching" popping up in the literature of the counseling profession and wondered whether this was just the "helping fad of the month" or if it might be a legitimate evolution within the helping professions. Deb began using coaching principles with some of her clients and soon found that it was second nature and more importantly, they worked! She read an article by Pat in *Practice Strategies,* and contacted him; a lasting and rewarding friendship and professional alliance blossomed. Deb retired from her university professorship in 1999 to focus on teaching and writing about life coaching.

Since our meeting, we have delivered national presentations on life coaching, collaborated on ideas for the development of the Institute of Life Coaching curriculum, and discussed more effective ways to share life coaching strategies with helping professionals who want more out of their lives and careers. The book you have before you is a product of our collegial relationship and dedication to training helping professionals to be effective life coaches. We want life coaching to become a household word and a service that is readily available to all who seek it.

Our intuitive belief that helping professionals were ready for a new way to do business has been constantly reinforced over the past several years as we have heard from increasing numbers of counselors, psychologists, and family therapists. As we reached out through books and journal articles and through presentations, the demand for more information about how therapists could transition into life coaching grew. It was clear that helping professionals wanted something more meaningful and satisfying and we believed, for many, life coaching could help meet that need.

---

*Coach University, founded by Thomas Leonard in the 1990s, was the first distance learning coach training program.

We wrote this book for therapists considering a career transition into life coaching. In other words, we wrote this book for you. We use the term "therapist" in our book to broadly define helping professionals whose academic preparation and training is in areas including family therapy, psychology, sociology, counseling, and even psychiatry. When we speak of therapists, we want you to know we are speaking to all trained helping professionals.

As you read, you will see that we firmly believe therapists are uniquely positioned to become outstanding life coaches. The transferable helping skills, which trained and experienced therapists bring to the coaching relationship, are extremely valuable in facilitating successful change and growth for coaching clients. We will discuss these skills later in the book and also speak to the specific transitions needed in the traditional model of helping in order to create a coaching, rather than therapeutic, relationship.

While there are numerous books on the market that write about some aspect of the coaching profession, many of the general coaching publications focus on business or corporate coaching. Our book takes into account the rich history that psychology has to offer and how professionals with backgrounds and training in the helping professions can transition their skills into a career as a life coach. Additionally, ours is one of the few with emphasis the whole person approach to coaching, which we call life coaching. Whether you are interested in exploring the coaching profession in general as a way to transform your practice, or if focused on life coaching, we believe you, as a trained helping professional, will find this book a valuable resource to support your transition.

What Is Life Coaching?

Therapists can renew their souls with life coaching. But what is life coaching? Here are some general definitions from three professional sources:

> Life coaches assist people to discover what they want in life and unlock their own brilliance to achieve it. Life coaching is about people generating their own answers, not looking outside of themselves for solutions. This process is not about teaching what you already know or about clients acting as students. Instead, life coaching is empowering people to invent something new—to think something they've never thought before and to say something they've never said before. (Ellis, 1998, p. 1, p. 3)

Coaching is a powerful relationship for people making important changes in their lives. (Whitworth, Kimsey-House, & Sandahl, 1998, p. xvii)

Coaching is an ongoing relationship, which focuses on clients taking action toward the realization of their visions, goals, or desires. Coaching uses a process of inquiry and personal discovery to build the client's level of awareness and responsibility and provides the client with structure, support, and feedback. The coaching process helps clients both define and achieve professional and personal goals faster and with more ease than would be possible otherwise. (International Coach Federation, from their Web site, www.coachfederation.org)

How we define life coaching has been the subject of much thought and discussion. As we present workshops across the country, we continue to revise and refine what we believe most captures the essence of life coaching. For us, it is vital that our definition include the following features, all of which we discuss in greater detail later.

The focus is on the future. Life coaching is about designing a future, not getting over a past.

The relationship is typically long-term. Life coaching, from our holistic model, is a relationship that lasts months and years rather than a short-term encounter for a brief, specific concern.

The goals, dreams, and visions (wants) drive the action. Helping clients to discover what they want (in all aspects of their lives) is an essential component of the life coaching relationship.

There are multiple paths to reach each want. In order to increase the likelihood of success, life coaches help clients create multiple paths to achieve what they want in their lives.

The client knows the way (even though he or she may not realize it at the time). The life coaches we train know that the answers and solutions rest with the client. Our goal is for clients to brilliantly create the life they have always wanted rather than have a coach tell them what they "should" or "need to" do in order to achieve what they want.

Here is our own definition of life coaching as it applies to the information we will present: Life coaching is a powerful human relationship where trained coaches assist people to design their future rather than get over their past. Through a typically long-term relationship, coaches aid clients in creating visions and goals for ALL aspects of their lives and creating multiple strategies to support achieving those goals. Coaches recognize the brilliance of each client and their personal power to discover their own solutions when provided with support, accountability and unconditional positive regard.

Life coaching can be challenging, as well as financially and spiritually rewarding. Making the transition from therapist to life coach requires a journey of self-exploration and self-awareness, as well as creative planning. We recognize from working with many therapists that life coaching is not for everyone. We also know that the therapists who bravely explore this new opportunity often find it just what they were seeking in their effort to renew their soul as helpers of the human spirit.

You will get the most out of this book if you actively participate. We've collected stories and quotes from therapists who have become life coaches. As you read them, record your own thoughts, concerns, or insights. We've also designed selected activities to help you get the most out of your exploration into life coaching. This book will serve as your guide whether life coaching specifically or coaching in general is your goal; we are confident that it provides many opportunities for you to consider new ways of offering your professional helping services.

The life coaching relationship focuses on what the client wants. Similarly, we encourage you to use the time you spend reading our book to consider *what you really want in your life*. We recognize that it is sometimes hard for helpers to take time for creating their own futures but we *really* want you to give attention to yourself, your wants, and your desires. Make a commitment to explore life coaching as a possible transition fully and completely. Give yourself to the process, clarify your desires, use effective creative planning, and you will be amazed at the results. As you read think of this question: *"What do I want my future as a helping professional to look like and is life coaching right for me?"*

Jeannine Wade, one of the therapists we trained as a life coach through our workshops and the Institute for Life Coach Training* (formerly Therapist

---

*The Institute for Life Coach Training, initially Therapist University, was founded by Dr. Patrick Williams in 1998 with the express purpose of providing coach training exclusively to the helping professions. It is one of the premier coach training programs, is internationally recognized, and delivers courses in the United States, Canada, and Europe. ILCT offers a comprehensive training program for the helping professions as well as a certification program.

University) wrote the following letter. Her words reflect her satisfaction in the choice she made and her empowerment from the transition.

> Two years ago, I was becoming aware that I was feeling very "burned out." I felt like I desperately needed to make some changes, but I didn't know how to begin. I thought, "I don't have enough time for what I need to do now—how can I find the time to make changes?"
>
> On the surface my life was good. I was healthy; I had a nice home, a good husband, and a successful private practice as a psychologist. I had a loving family and friends. But something was missing. And I felt like I didn't have the time to slow down long enough to figure out what it was. I just knew I felt I had too many responsibilities and not enough time; too many details overwhelming me and not enough joy and fun. I had not allowed myself the choice to make my life better.
>
> Then I went to the national meeting of marriage and family therapists in Dallas. The first session I chose to attend was "Adding Coaching to Your Private Practice." I had heard of personal coaching, but I didn't really know what it was.
>
> In that session, two things happened for me. First, I realized that I could change my life for the better—here was someone not only saying it was okay, but also that there was a whole new field to help me do just that. When I think about it now, it is hard to believe that as much as I was helping others change their lives, I wasn't allowing myself to accept that I could change mine.
>
> And second, I realized that being a part of this new field made me feel excited in a way that I hadn't felt in a long time. It seemed to fit with everything I had been working toward in my life, including the way I did therapy—which is helping the individual: to listen to themselves, to believe that they can make their lives better, and to take the steps to make their dreams a reality.
>
> Now, two years later, after having my own coach and becoming a coach, my life is very different. I have made many changes that have helped, and I continue to make changes. The biggest change is the belief that I can make my life what I want it to be, and one of my greatest joys is helping others to do the same.

Jeannine represents hundreds of therapists who have made the choice to either add coaching to their therapy business or become full-time life coaches. We'll share more of their stories later on. For now, here is an overview of where we are headed. Part I, Why Life Coaching? explores the history of the coaching movement and why we believe society is hungry for life coaches. Part II, Life Coaching for Therapists, examines its similarities and distinctions with therapy, discusses the coaching relationship, and considers some of the skills therapists will need to learn and unlearn in order to reclaim their joyfulness. Part III, Powerful Transition Tools, describes getting started as a life coach and the specific tools therapists need in the life coaching relationship and in establishing a successful life coaching practice. Part IV, Expanding your Coaching Practice, offers alternatives to the basic life coaching model, self-care strategies for life coaches, and peeks into the future of life coaching. Question and Answer and Resources sections follow part IV.

So, as we move to part I, remember to sit with that very important question mentioned earlier: "What do I want my future as a helping professional to look like and is life coaching right for me?"

Therapist as Life Coach
Transforming Your Practice

PART I
Why Life Coaching?

CHAPTER ONE

Why Therapists As Life Coaches?

You see things, and you say, "Why?" But I dream things
that never were; and I say, "Why not?"
                                        —George Bernard Shaw

Around 1990, there was little mention of coaching except in the corporate culture. Mentoring and executive coaching was something that many top managers and CEOs utilized, either informally from a colleague or formally by hiring a consultant or psychologist who became their executive coach. We will elaborate on the history of coaching more in chapter 2, but, for now, let us examine why life coaching is becoming more popularized and prevalent.

The International Coach Federation was founded in 1992 but did not have a real presence until its first convention in 1996. They have kept detailed archives of media coverage on coaching since the early 1990s. There were two newspaper articles in 1993, four in 1994 (including one from Australia) and seven in 1995. The majority of articles appeared in publications from the United States. Then, in 1996, a huge increase in publicity occurred with more than 60 articles, television interviews, and radio shows on the topic of coaching. Every year since, the media coverage has increased to hundreds of articles and live media coverage, both national and local radio and television such as "Good Morning America," "Today," etc., each year throughout the United States, Europe, Australia, Canada, Japan, Singapore, and other countries. In addition, the only books written about coaching before the 1990s were geared to corporate and performance coaching. Now there are several good recent books about life coaching; a few are national best-sellers. Laura

Berman Fortgang (1998) and Cheryl Richardson (1998, 2000), both professional life coaches, have been frequent guests on "Oprah." Cheryl is now a regular monthly guest on "Oprah" as a life makeover coach. Life coaching as a phenomenon originated in the United States and has spread worldwide. Coaching will soon reach a critical mass in society where people will have heard of coaching, know when they need a coach, know how to find a coach, and know the difference between partnering with a life coach versus seeking the services of a therapist or counselor.

Society Is Changing

We believe that this new profession has emerged out of a major shift in societal parameters. Alvin Toffler wrote the now-famous book *Future Shock* in 1970. It was the most popular publication of its time to speak about the phenomenon of how rapid change impacted the human condition and its societal structures. His warnings and descriptions now seem underestimated in comparison with the exponential speed of change that society now experiences.

We both grew up in the 1950s—then society seemed predictable and stable. People generally stayed married, went to college for four years, and kept their careers for life if not most of their life. There was little emphasis on adult education, career transitions, or moving so far from home or as often as we do today. Company loyalty was big; you worked 30 years or so, got your "gold watch," and had a retirement party. But the times and society have both changed. Now the younger generation's motto is "Have résumé will travel!" For the baby boomer generation, the trend is to be self-employed or well-invested and able to be very mobile and entrepreneurial.

In the 1950s and the decades before World War II, there were few therapists or counselors because the profession was just emerging. Now there are well over 500,000 licensed therapists in the United States. In the 1950s, people went to Uncle Charley, their clergy, or their grandparents for counsel or had mentors in the workplace. Today, mentors are not as easily available with the decrease in lifelong communities—the quiet neighborhoods of the past where everyone knew everyone else and neighbors, especially older people, could be informal mentors and "sages." Constant career changes have also impacted the availability of mentoring.

In the 1970s and 1980s, when corporate America began the great downsizing experiment, the middle manager became a dinosaur and was replaced by work teams, self-management, and trickle-down edicts from executive management. The middle manager had been the mentor, coach, and go-between for employees and the top management of the company. As the middle manager disappeared, so did the natural mentoring that was available to employees. People, both in the workplace and in their personal lives, lost their listeners and their confidantes. During this period, consultants thrived. Companies hired consultants to come in and offer training packages that gave an outside voice and a seemingly objective ear to address the employees' morale, absenteeism, conflict, and relationship struggles in a work team or department. Consultants were viewed as both a necessary evil and a competitive edge.

Today, change is the norm and both entrepreneurism and isolation, even in a corporate culture, are the result. Additionally, there are more self-employed and home-office workers than ever before and this trend is growing exponentially. With global communications, virtual technology, e-mail, voice mail and wireless office technology, we are an entrepreneurial and mobile workforce. In fact, as Judy Feld, a friend and Pat's first coach, writes in her SOHO Success Letter™ (SOHO stands for Small Office/Home Office) (1998), "growth of the alternative workplace will continue. This is not a fad. Current estimates place 30–40 million people in the USA as either telecommunters or home-based workers." Millions of workers can now conduct their business away from office buildings and can live almost anywhere they choose. This trend has forever changed the traditional nature of the "workplace."

Why People Need Life Coaches

Society has gone from being stable and mostly predictable to being fast-paced, impersonal, and constantly evolving. As mentioned earlier, with such swift change in all aspects of life and the loss of mentors for most people, life coaching becomes the new profession where one can hire a mentor as their personal coach. Carl Rogers once said that psychotherapy was often like "buying a friend"; hiring a coach is a way to buy a mentor and guide that one cannot easily find. Similarly, having a coach has become a sought-after employee benefit in many companies and for those that are self-employed, a coach is someone to keep them focused, connected to their desired outcomes, and living their life "on purpose."

There are many types of coaching available to people today and, as the profession grows, mental health therapists will be able to fill many specialty niches, such as *relationship coaching, parenting coaching, teen coaching, family business coaching,* etc. In the corporate arena, *executive coaching* is popular and prevalent but often focuses primarily on work goals and work teams, not necessarily whole life coaching with, as we say, "the person behind the job." Because more and more people are getting more interested in having a life *and* a job, companies are discovering that coaching can lead to more balanced, vibrant, and happy employees, and that leads to less turnover, better working relationships, and increased productivity and efficiency. With all the pressures from society and its lack of stability and predictability, a coach becomes someone who can assist the client in being a *change master.*

A well-trained and experienced life coach may also refer the client to other coaching specialists as needed or requested. To be certain, a corporate or executive coach needs some special training for the uniqueness of the corporate world, but often coaches with other skills can be used for specific goals. We have referred our individual clients to relationship coaches when our client and his or her spouse needed some relationship guidance. Likewise, other coaches (acting as the personal life coach) have referred to specialized coaches for clients who needed tips on getting a book published, help with financial planning, or advice on how to deal with an unruly teenager. General life coaching can continue or be resumed after the referral coaching is complete. A life coach is the one person who is central to the client's life and with whom he or she cannot work, live, or sleep. The life coach can be the person who keeps a client focused, motivated, purposeful, and accountable.

Why Therapists Can Make Great Life Coaches

Successful coaches come from a myriad of professional backgrounds. Business and professional consultants, human resources managers, organizational consultants, entrepreneurs, and marketing specialists are a few of the careers that coaches might have had before adding coaching to their résumé. For the purpose of this book, we want to discuss those unique skills trained and experienced helping professionals bring to life coaching relationships. The following list highlights some of the reasons we believe therapists are uniquely qualified for making the transition into life coaching.

1. Skillful listening. Deep and empathic listening is at the heart of the therapeutic relationship, and helping professionals have had much professional experience honing their listening skills. In addition to listening, they are able to hear what is not being said and to detect how nuances of expression, voice, and energy unite or contradict what the client is saying with their nonverbal cues. However, therapists would have to "unlearn" the tendency to analyze and dig into the past in order to be successful coaches.

2. Gift of reframing. The skill of putting a positive or less innocuous spin on a statement or belief expressed by a client is critical to effective life coaching. For example, a client might be distraught over not getting her desired promotion. The reframe might be to ask her to consider what she can learn from the experience and to mention that maybe there is a greater opportunity in the future. Turning problems into opportunities is one way to use reframing as a coaching skill. You put the belief into a new "frame" thereby changing the perspective of the statement or belief toward positive thinking.

3. Ability to suspend judgment. Helping professionals have heard it all! They can listen to "truth telling" from their clients and not be shocked. Most of the time, what client's need to be truthful about is not earth-shattering, except to them. Having a place to "dump" frustration or anxiety and express their deepest desires or fear, as in the coaching relationship, is very freeing.

4. Experience with confidentiality and ethics. Professional therapists already respect confidentiality and have strong ethical guidelines. In fact, the boundaries and professional guidelines in therapy are so strong, coaches will actually find that clients, since they are not generally emotionally fragile, are much looser with their own boundaries. Coaching clients are proud to have a coach and will not keep that a secret. However, the trained therapist-turned-coach will err on the side of strict confidentiality until clear guidance by the client redefines the expectations.

5. Ability to seek solutions and think of possibilities. Trained and experienced therapists are typically good solution seekers and possibility thinkers and their professional training and experience has undoubtedly enhanced these skills. This is especially true for therapists who have embraced humanistic and client-centered paradigms, including the recent advances in solution-focused therapy.

These are the five unique skills that experienced therapists bring to the coaching profession. Eventually, of course, the goal of masterful coaching is to digest the techniques, add new skills, and reach a level of comfort just being a coach, more than just doing coaching!

How Therapists Become Life Coaches

If a therapist or counselor chooses to add life coaching to her practice, she can easily market her services nationally and even internationally with the practice of telephone coaching. There are many therapists who now offer therapy and counseling services via the Internet or telephone. While we do not want to go into an extended discussion of teletherapy here, we believe that it can be risky depending on the client. Coaching should be done with mature, responsible persons. Therapy should be done in person with occasional phone sessions when the person is not at risk or emotionally fragile. Adding coaching to your practice allows your business to grow geographically—you can live where you want without licensing concerns, and you can even travel and still be in contact with your coaching clients. The hourly fees also are higher than usual and customary therapy fees and clients pay by a monthly "retainer" often for several months if not years. Coaching clients stay for the long haul because they *want* to, not because they *need* to.

Characteristics of Successful Coaches

So, as we already mentioned, life coaching is appealing to helping professionals who want to either add coaching to their business or move into coaching full-time (to which one can still include training, consulting, speaking, and writing). Most therapists are generally "people persons" meaning they like people, are pleasant, relate well with others, and want clients to have more fulfilling lives. But, as we all know, there are therapists who make us wonder how they stay in business—they either don't have effective professional personalities or business sense, or both.

We have found through our anecdotal research and experience with the hundreds of therapists we have trained that those who are drawn to coaching tend to share some important characteristics. You will notice that these also apply to well-adjusted, masterful therapists.

1. They are well-adjusted and constantly seek personal improvement or development.
2. They have a lightness of being and *joie de vivre*.
3. They are passionate about "growing" people.
4. They understand the distinction and balance between *being* and *doing*.
5. They are able to suspend judgment and stay open-minded.
6. They are "risk takers" willing to get out of their comfort zone.
7. They are entrepreneurial—even if they do not have great business skills they are visionaries, able to see the big picture and reinvent themselves and their business to meet current trends.
8. They want to have a life *and* a business.
9. They have a worldview and a more globalistic vision.
10. They are naturally motivational and optimistic.
11. They are great listeners who are able to empathize with their clients.
12. They are mentally healthy and resilient when life knocks them down.
13. Their focus is on developing the future, not fixing the past.
14. They are able to collaborate and partner with their clients, shedding the "expert" role.
15. They have a willingness to believe in the brilliance or potential for greatness in all people.
16. They look at possibilities instead of problems and causes (as do solution-focused therapists).
17. They exude confidence, even when unsure.
18. They present as more authentic and genuine, with high integrity.
19. They are willing to say, "I don't know," and explore where and how to learn what is needed.
20. They enjoy what they do and are enthusiastic and passionate about life.

So, as life coaching grows as a newly defined profession, many therapists with the above characteristics will recognize that they have been coaches for a long time, they just did not know what to call it! We strongly believe that the paradigm and powerfulness of coaching will attract more healthy clients than therapy did and, in fact, many of the "problems in living" that clients sought the assistance of a therapist for are better served by a life coach, avoiding the stigma of therapy altogether.

While there may be a new word developed in the future for the coaching relationship, the term life coach (or personal coach) fits very well right now.

Other terms like personal consultant, life strategist, etc., seem to be too vague and constrained.

We believe that life coaching is part of a larger paradigm shift toward people wanting to live their lives more purposefully. This could be called a movement away from the paradigm of pathology to the paradigm of possibility. There are many reasons that one could cite beyond the scope of this book, but life coaching has evolved because it makes sense to people today to have a partner who will elicit their unique greatness and who will assist them to move from mediocrity to excellence in living. Life coaching exists because it is helpful, and it will prosper because it is transformational.

CHAPTER TWO

The History and Evolution of Life Coaching

*Change is the law of life, and those who look only to the past
or the present are certain to miss the future.*
            —John F. Kennedy

Historical information provides current and prospective life coaches with
both a framework for understanding their profession and insight into future
opportunities. This framework also helps life coaches place themselves
squarely within the larger context of a profession that is still developing,
changing, and evolving. As we cast our eyes across the diverse threads of the
past, perhaps we will come to understand the present more accurately and
will be better prepared as life coaching enters the twenty-first century. We
believe an examination of the evolution of life coaching also helps therapists
to make the transition to life coaching by further clarifying the similarities
and differences between life coaching and other helping professions.

Systematic literature reviews and comprehensive historical accounts of the
development of life coaching have not been conducted. We know of only
one source, *The Handbook of Coaching* by Frederic Hudson (1999), that has
included historical content as part of the more extended treatment of other
life coaching–related topics. No books on coaching have focused exclusively
on the development of life coaching from its roots in modern psychology
and counseling theories. This is an area that is ripe for life coaching scholars
interested in publishing opportunities.

The professional literature in business and human resource development
refers to coaching as it developed in organizations (Hargrove, 1995; Whitmore, 1996), but documentation of the evolution of coaching, specifically life

coaching, in the context of the helping professions is scant. Psychological theories (Freud, 1965; Hudson, 1999; Jung, 1953, 1976) of adult development, including psychosocial stage theories and the social theories of adult development, do offer opportunities for in-depth study for readers seeking a deeper theoretical perspective. Similarly, review of solution-focused therapy strategies and narrative therapy techniques (with which most therapists are already well acquainted) provides the reader with examples of psychotherapy techniques that develop the competence of the client. In fact, Bill O'Hanlon, who is the author of more than a dozen books on solution-focused counseling approaches, suggested in a conversation with Pat that we not use the term "psychotherapy" and see it instead as "possibility counseling." And John Walter and Jane Peller (2000) boldly declare that psychotherapy should be called "personal consulting." That sounds like life coaching to us. These theorists and other modernists actually are stressing a nonpathological context for counseling. However, they really refer to using coachlike skills with a therapy or counseling client. We want you to see that a life coaching relationship with a client is very distinct from just using coaching skills. It is a unique professional relationship in which one explores with their coach (over time) how to live their life more fully and "on purpose." The Resources section at the end of this book provides suggestions for future reading and exploration.

The Evolution of Coaching Terminology

When we started our coaching careers, people would often ask, "What sport do you coach?" This is not surprising, given the history of the word "coach" and its tie to athletics. Now, when we say "life coach," they still look at us curiously, but we no longer need to discuss "what sport." Our profession is receiving more and more public awareness and attention. And if they do ask, "What sport?" we can answer, "The game of life!"

Coaching and mentoring have been common terms in the corporate environment for decades. Executive coaching has always been accepted as a perk or desirable form of consultation and support for high-level management. A distinction today, however, is mentoring, which is a service provided formally or informally in order to train those employees who might be moving up the corporate ladder internally and are mentored on the manager's ways. Corporate coaching today is provided both internally (by coaches who work for the company) and externally (by coaches hired either by the company or the managers themselves). Life coaching, however, has become desirable and accessible to those outside the corporate environment.

The Psychological Roots of Life Coaching

Psychological theorists in the early part of the twentieth century set the framework for life coaching's "whole and healthy person" view. The shift from seeing clients as ill or pathological toward viewing them as "well and whole" and seeking a richer life is paramount to understanding the evolution of life coaching. Life coaches view clients as whole and brilliant persons and focus not on pathology, but on wellness.

Most people would agree that Sigmund Freud had a dramatic influence on society's view of mental illness and a deeper understanding of behavior. While much of Freud's theory has little applicability to life coaching, he did profess that driving influences in people's lives were not conscious (ego-driven) but unconscious forces—the id (libido) and the superego (social conscience), which he believed were symbols for analysis and dream interpretation. It is this emphasis on symbolic thinking that is beneficial for life coaching. Life coaches help clients discover their brilliance, which often lies masked or buried in their unconsciousness and can be experienced when they begin to design their lives consciously and purposely.

But colleagues from Freud's inner circle, such as Carl Jung and Alfred Adler, broke away from his theories of neuroses and psychosis and posited theories that were more teleological and optimistic about human potential. Although there remains a significant distinction between therapy approaches and coaching (which we will discuss later in-depth) many of Adler and Jung's theories are antecedents to modern-day life coaching.

Adler, for example, saw himself as more of a personal educator, believing that every person develops a unique life approach, which shapes his or her goals, values, habits, and personal drives. He believed that happiness arises from a sense of significance and social connectedness (belonging), not merely individual objectives and desires. Adler saw each person as the creator and artist of his or her life and frequently involved his clients in goal setting, life planning, and inventing their future—all tenets and approaches in life coaching today.

Similarly, Carl Jung believed in the power of connectedness and relationships, as well as a "future orientation" or teleological belief that we create our futures through visioning and purposeful living. Jung's writings really focused on life after the age of 40 and he concentrated on many of the life issues of our later years. This is particularly appropriate for life coaches because we work primarily with adult learners. Jung often coached adults through a "life review" and encouraged his clients to consciously live their lives by expressing their natural gifts and talents and moving toward self-individuation by living life "on purpose."

Jung's theories and approaches also emphasized spirituality and values expressed as one goes though the process he called individuation—the progression and development of the spiritual self. This is particularly prevalent in the second half of life, a time when life coaches are most likely to experience this themselves and with their clients. Jung also described the importance of myths and rituals, which are increasingly becoming important components of our life coaching clients' lives. We believe therapist-trained coaches are particularly qualified to assist clients in these important stages of adult development.

The Boulder Conference: Psychology Comes of Age

Clinical psychology, as a profession separate from research and academia, was catapulted into the latter half of the twentieth century because of the historical Boulder Conference in 1949 —the first national meeting ever held in the United States to discuss standards of graduate training in psychology, despite the fact that doctoral programs in America had been around more than 60 years (Albee, 2000). Up to that point, the emphasis was on theory and human behavior, not so much on clinical or psychotherapeutic applications in a systemized, integrated approach. The demand for psychologists and counselors grew after World War II for treating posttraumatic stress, the psychological impact of war injuries, and the military's need to prepare soldiers with improved emphasis on mental health and the hope for a kind of "stress inoculation." Looking back now at the Boulder Conference, it is easy to see that the teaching of clinical psychology included much of what today is found in counseling psychology and even the offshoots of counseling and marriage and family therapy.

Influences of Humanistic Psychology and the Human Potential Movement

During this time period, counseling and psychotherapy actually were starting to be viewed by many as arts more than sciences. The influence of the theories of Maslow (1968, 1970, 1971) and the emergence of humanistic, client-centered approaches (Bugenthal, 1967; Fadiman & Frager, 1976; Frankl, 1959; Rogers, 1951; among others) saw the client as full of potential and possibility rather than as one with neuroses or pathology.

In 1951, Carl Rogers's book, *Client-Centered Therapy* really defined counseling and therapy as relationships in which the client was assumed to have the ability to change and grow by the clinician creating a therapeutic alliance. This alliance evolved from a safe, confidential space granting the client or patient what Rogers called *unconditional positive regard.* We believe this shift in perspective was a significant precursor to what is called life coaching today.

In the years after World War II, American psychologists began to be influenced by European schools of thought, namely phenomenology and existentialism. These points of view layed much of the philosophical foundation for what was to become the Third Force* in psychological thought, humanistic psychology. (The early work of Carl Rogers, Kurt Lewin, Prescott Lecky, and, eventually, Abraham Maslow also served as great influences.) Emphasis is now on studying the whole person, not fragmented parts. Although the philosophies and values of humanistic psychology unified the whole field of psychology, it also polarized the profession. Humanistic psychology arose largely as a reaction against behaviorism's mechanistic view of humanity and was once again concerned with human experience and intrapsychic motivations as it had been in psychology's earliest years, but these concerns were viewed as nonobservable, nonmeasurable, intervening variables according to behavioral psychology's precepts.

Abraham Maslow, considered by many the father of humanistic psychology, was largely responsible for injecting much credibility and energy into the human potential movement of the sixties with the publication of his seminal treatise, *Toward a Psychology of Being* (1968). In this work, Maslow summarized his research of "self actualizing people" (a term first coined by Kurt Goldstein) and coined terms such as "full-humanness" and wrote about "being" and "becoming." This book is largely a continuation of theories he first posited in *Motivation and Personality* (1954, 1987). Maslow studied the "healthy personality" of people who he termed *self-actualizers*; he researched, questioned, and observed people who were living with a sense

---

*There are Four Forces: the First Force is Freudian psychology; the Second Force is behavioral psychology; the Third Force is humanistic psychology; and the Fourth Force is transpersonal psychology.

of vitality and purpose and who were constantly seeking to grow psycho-logically and achieve more of their human potential. It is this key point in history that we believe set the framework for the field of life coaching to emerge in the '90s. Persons seeking personal evolution and ways to live their life more fully do not need psychological counseling; life coaching is a more accurate paradigm for the improved outcomes or achievements the client seeks.

Maslow was instrumental in giving great value and importance to the idea of personal growth and its necessity for the healthy personality. However, Maslow was not the first with these ideas. Many early psychiatrists and psy-chologists revolted against the orthodox approaches to mental problems and their emphasis on the person's pathological or pathogenic components. The reader has already been introduced to the influential work of Adler and Jung, but Gordon Allport, James Bugental, Kurt Goldstein, Karen Horney, Sidney Jourard, Prescott Lecky, Rollo May, Carl Rogers also influenced psychology's move toward a wellness perspective that laid much of the groundwork for modern coaching theory, perspective, and techniques.

Third Force Psychology has found its place in mainstream psychology and is represented by an international organization. The first issue of the *Journal of Humanistic Psychology* was published in 1961 and edited by Anthony Sutich. The Association of Humanistic Psychology (AHP) began the follow-ing year. Abraham Maslow's ideas were central to the beginnings of both the journal and the association, but the AHP was not organized simply to promote his philosophy. The AHP represents a broad viewpoint, but it emerged as the third major force (after Freudianism and behaviorism) in psy-chology because of its unitary revolt against mechanistic, deterministic psy-chology. We believe this philosophical shift took root in a generation that now rejects the idea of sickness and seeks wellness, wholeness, and pur-poseful living instead. Hence the emergence of life coaching!

Influences of Milton Erickson and Solution-focused Approaches

The work of Milton Erickson (the father of American hypnosis) is a key pre-cursor to the methods in coaching today. Milton Erickson, an iconoclastic and unique psychiatrist, believed in the inherent ability of individuals to achieve wellness if the reason for an illness could be thwarted. Erickson often achieved seemingly "miraculous results" from just a few sessions with a patient. Jay Haley (1986) coined the term "uncommon therapy" to describe Erickson's approach.

Bandler and Grindler (1975), who were students of Erickson, then developed the approach called neuro-linguistic programming (NLP), which is an evolution of much of Ericksonian theory and technique. This system focused on outcome for the client and on powerful use of language and question-asking by the therapist to facilitate transformational change. Linguistics and inquiry are key aspects of the work of a life coach, and much of the heritage lies in the early work of Ericksonian practitioners.

More recent psychological approaches that have evolved from Ericksonian and other wellness approaches are the solution-focused therapies. These approaches are not insight- or depth psychology–dependent and are also powerful influences on modern coaching practices and theory. Most notably, Glasser's reality therapy, Ellis's rational emotive therapy, systemic family therapies (Haley, Madanes, Satir), neuro-linguistic programming (NLP) (Bandler and Grindler), psychosynthesis (Assagioli), and many other hybrids of these lend themselves to coaching strategies. In all of these, the main focus is not pathology but behavior change through increased awareness and choices to allow for desired future results and solutions to current "problems in living." For example, the work of Bill O'Hanlon (1999a) emphasizes possibilities and preferencing—an approach that fits well in life coaching relationships. The modern approaches of Steve de Shazer (1988) and his colleagues called solution-focused counseling could just as easily be called coaching. In fact, many of their techniques and approaches for difficult clients have been adapted into coaching techniques, such as the miracle question and asking powerful questions that lead to action-oriented steps.

Life coaching has really developed from three streams: (1) helping professions such as psychotherapy and counseling and related theoretical perspectives as noted above, (2) consulting and organizational development and industrial psychology, and (3) personal development training such as EST, Lifespring, Landmark Forum, and Anthony Robbins.

The personal development courses listed above all focus on taking personal action and responsibility for one's life choices. They often include one-to-one coaching as part of their service or recommend it to those who desire sustainable results from the weekend training experience.

The Curse of the Medical Model

Unfortunately, somewhere along the way, the helping professions (spear-headed by clinical psychology) adopted, or were co-opted by, the medical model. The medical model sees the client as being ill, as a patient with a diagnosis in need of treatment or symptom relief. While there clearly are some serious mental illnesses that benefit from clinical psychology or skillful psychotherapy, many people in the past were treated and labeled for what were really "problems in living"—situations or circumstances that did not need a diagnosis or assumption of pathology. Persons in the past seeking personal growth typically had nowhere to turn but to therapists, seminars, or self-help books. Sadly, many of these seminars and books also were problem-focused rather than looking forward for the powerful strategies of healthy life design.

Today, many clinicians find themselves on a dead-end street blocked by a corporate managed health care system where the main concern is financial profit, not mental health delivery. Unfortunately, most diagnoses pathologized people who weren't really mentally ill. These diagnoses became part of clients' permanent medical records, leading to embarrassment, insurance rejection, and other unnecessary problems. We believe society is ready for life coaching in which a relationship is sought to create a future—not to get over a past—and certainly not to get a diagnosis for their effort.

Again, we believe psychotherapy and counseling can treat diagnosable mental illnesses and are effective (although the research on this point is disconcerting). However, these longer-term treatments (if you expect insurance to foot the bills) are often viewed as too expensive. Increasingly, the benefits of a relationship, in which change and insight occur over time, are not supported in the medical model. The counseling professions, in our opinion, fell into a trap after adopting the medical model and third-party payment for services. Now, in order to survive, counselors and therapists are reducing fees and psychologists are even trying to obtain prescription privileges for psychotropic drugs, moving further into the medical arena. G. W. Albee (1998) says that psychologists (and therefore other therapists) have "sold their souls to the Devil: the disease model of mental disorders" (pp. 247–248).

Professional Associations and Growth of the Coaching Industry

As you have read, the influences of many psychological theorists and practitioners from the turn of the century to now have contributed to the development and evolution of the field of life coaching.

Telecoaching—where coaches and clients talk by phone—was largely created and developed by an ingenious visionary named Thomas Leonard. In 1992, Thomas Leonard founded Coach University, which trained persons who wanted to learn to be coaches through classes taught by teleconference and enjoy the portability and "live and work anywhere" possibilities of telecoaching. At about the same time, Laura Whitworth, with the help of several colleagues, founded the Coaches Training Institute in San Francisco, which trains coaches through a series of weekend workshops and follow-up training by telephone. In 1995, Whitworth and her colleagues also founded the Personal and Professional Coaches Association (PPCA), and in 1996, Thomas Leonard initiated the creation of the International Coach Federation, largely supported by Coach University. In 1996, the first annual ICF convention was held in Houston, Texas with about 200 persons in attendance. In 1997, the second annual ICF convention had over 300 in attendance and Sandy Vilas (owner of Coach U) and Laura Whitworth (president of PPCA) announced the merger of the ICF and the PPCA into one body (The International Coach Federation)—membership has grown exponentially since then. In 2002 there are (2000) over 14,000 members worldwide. Today there are more than four-dozen identified coach training schools but only a handful that specialize in training mental health therapists.

Coach Training Opportunities

Prior to the development of the several coach training opportunities available today for this new profession, coaching was a term primarily used in the arts (voice coaches, drama coaches), athletic, and corporate worlds. Now, coaching is seen as both valuable and convenient to the general professional for assistance in total life design. Due to the formal training available to prospective coaches who come from a variety of disciplines and work experiences, the general public can now find a personal coach who is well-trained to assist them in achieving the big goals and desires of their personal and professional lives.

Life coaching is a twentieth-century phenomenon with roots in early psychological theories. It is a profession still experiencing dynamic growth and change. Life coaching will no doubt continue to interact developmentally with social, economic, and political processes, draw on the knowledge base of diverse disciplines, enhance its intellectual and professional maturity, and continue to establish itself internationally and domestically. Cooperative efforts among diverse professional groups will enable life coaching to develop in more unified and collaborative ways in order to strengthen its influence.

CHAPTER THREE

The Courage to Begin

We gain a powerful perspective when we courage what we choose to do even when we feel afraid. Courage means accepting our feelings and sticking with our planned purposeful action.

—Dave Ellis

From the day you realize you want more out of your life as a helper, every step you take to explore life coaching is a step closer to becoming the person you really want to be. We believe you can have what you want and that life coaching is a great way to get it. All you need is the courage to begin.

We have shared the stories of how we personally made this major life change and offered you insights into our transitions. There were times along the way that we analyzed our decisions, when we found ourselves fearful about making this change. Change always requires strength and determination, therefore, being clear about what you want and what your purpose is essential. Our search to renew our souls and our practices has been rewarded by finding enhanced meaning in our work as helpers and the remarkable joy of discovering that who we are now as life coaches is even better than who we were as therapists.

Similarly, this is the story of people like you who we have met on our journey, such as therapists from workshops and conferences, people who call because they know someone we coached, faculty who have read our publications and are interested in the profession, and students in the Institute for Life Coach training program. It is about helping professionals, just like you, who have laughed and cried and dreamed with us. This chapter tells the stories of their personal transition experiences in order to help you find the courage to begin.

What Do You Want?

When we speak to groups of therapists who are interested in becoming coaches, they often reflect wistfully on their years working in a full rewarding practice where their insurance payments flowed freely, their appointment books were full, and their communities held them in high regard as valued and needed professionals. Nostalgia floats through the room and heads nod in agreement as these therapists speak.

> My first five years out of graduate school were the best. I entered a group practice with three other therapists. It took awhile but, with their referrals, my practice started filling. Most of my clients had insurance and were delighted with my skills as a therapist. I really felt like I was making a difference.

> One thing I loved about the 'good ole days' was my ability to work with the clients I really wanted to and felt I could help the most. It was challenging and stimulating. I looked forward to going into my office every day.

> Back before we were the joke of TV sitcoms, there was a mystery to being a psychologist and I kind of liked it that way. I felt like the community respected us as professionals and that felt good.

The wistfulness vanishes quickly when we ask therapists to describe what is changing in their practices that causes them to consider life coaching as a career transition. The climate in the room shifts dramatically and body language alters.

> I can't practice therapy, I'm too busy with the record keeping the darn managed care organization requires of me. There isn't time to fill out the paperwork, let alone see the clients. A simple intake

requires seven different forms and a call to the insurance company. Is this what I got my degree for?

Most days I find my successes with clients overwhelmed by the frustrations of doing HMO paper work. I know I'm a good therapist and I can make a difference, but it isn't fun any more.

Those therapists who have operated within the medical model frequently describe their practices as being increasingly buried under the piles of paper generated by the managed care machine. No longer, they wail, does insurance support the therapy they believe their clients need or at least deserve.

I made seven calls and sent three sets of summary notes to the case review person before finally getting authorization to see this couple for two additional visits. By the time I called the couple back with the news, they were separated and one had left the state. I don't know, maybe it wouldn't have made a difference but what it did do was take away my faith in this system of care.

Many describe facing choices between working under the shackles of a "bottom line," "profit hungry" insurance company or being pushed into trying to find enough clients who will pay out-of-pocket to sustain their floundering practices.

I know I need to expand my practice; I've got a daughter going to college next year. Over the past three years I've seen my third-party payment receipts decline dramatically. But there are only so many hours in the day. How am I ever going to meet the bills without working fifty or sixty hours a week?

Look, I'm a therapist, not a businessman. People say we need to be 'entrepreneurs' and generate more clients who will pay our full fee but I hate that stuff. I can't go to a Rotary club and market myself like a car salesman. It's just not me.

At this point in a workshop, feelings of sadness, anger, frustration, and fear float so thickly in the room it feels like you can cut the air with a knife. Even those not caught up in the medical model describe feeling restless, wanting more, wanting to make a bigger difference.

> I just feel like there has to be more than what I'm doing now. I don't hate going to work but it doesn't excite me very often any more. There has to be a better way to do this.

It is painful to observe the looks on the faces of new professionals just starting their careers. They describe wondering how they will ever be able to make a fruitful living as therapists when those with far greater experience and training seem disillusioned and struggling.

> I remember hearing some of my graduate faculty talking in hushed tones about the bleak market for new professionals. I didn't believe it was possible.

> How am I ever going to make it? We want to get married when I finish my degree next summer but I'm starting to worry about how much money I'll make as a therapist. I never really worried about it before but when I see people with far more experience than I have saying they aren't happy with their income streams and practices, I start to panic. Maybe I should have gone into computers.

Now, before you get too depressed, take a few moments and think about why you are considering a transition from therapy to life coaching. What about your current situation causes *you* to consider a change in how you operate as a helping professional? It is time to get personal. Make a list of five or more things you would like to change about your current situation.

Things that frustrate me about my current practice as a therapist are:

1.
2.
3.
4.
5.

Have more than five? Go ahead and add them to your list but don't go on all day, there is a lot more to discuss!

The concerns we have recorded from therapists and the items that you have probably listed are pervasive at every workshop we present and every time we discuss life coaching options individually with therapists. Here is a list of typical concerns

1. Too many restrictions from insurance companies
2. Not enough clients
3. Not enough income
4. Lack of fulfillment
5. Don't know what to do to make it better

Therapists are usually very clear about what they *don't* like about their current situations and what they *don't* want to keep doing. It is easy to find a group of pessimistic therapists who are frustrated and exhausted. However, our experience is that many of the therapists in our workshops and our life coaching clients are challenged when faced with the change required to get what they *do* want. This is where you really need the courage to begin.

The TRY IT! Exercises

In this book, we will present an assortment of ideas and exercises; we ask that you try *all* of them. We have based these ideas and exercises on what has worked for our coaching clients and what has been successful in our workshops. Just *suspend your judgment* and give them a try. If they work, great. If a particular one doesn't seem to fit, don't worry, a different one will. Again, our request is simple, just *try* them!

Surprisingly, some people have a difficult time with this request. They want to analyze each exercise (this is especially true of therapists). If the idea conflicts with a way they have done things in the past, sometimes they just want to reject it. We do not want you to limit your ideas only to those you use now or you will finish this book in the same place you started. Also, if you limit your opportunity to try new things, you limit your potential to rediscover the creative energies inside you.

Dave Ellis, a professional colleague and friend of ours, has a great metaphor for what we are talking about. His super book, *Becoming a Master Student* (1999), presents many fantastic tools and strategies to help students succeed in college. One concept that fits perfectly for life coaching is the concept that "ideas are tools." For example, when you use a new hammer, you might notice its shape, weight, and balance, but you do not analyze the hammer or try to figure out if the hammer is "right" for you—you just use it.

If it works, you will use it again. If it doesn't work, then you find a new hammer. You do not have to *like* or even *agree* with the hammer as the tool of choice. Just *suspend judgment* and *TRY IT!*

This is what we are asking you to do throughout this book. When we present a new idea or want you to take on an assignment we believe will be a successful tool, we will precede the task with this header—TRY IT! Are you ready to try some new tools to help you become a great life coach?

TRY IT!

Since you are reading this and not on the phone with us once a week as our coaching client, we want to make sure there is a record of your progress through this experience. (Yes, we are confident you *will* make progress.) Therefore, we want you to get a journal so you can record your thoughts and ideas as well as set some goals for your life coaching career.

Treat yourself to a journal that feels like you. Take a special shopping trip to find one with the right design, texture, color, shape, and paper. Do you want lined or unlined paper? Do you want a pocket-size journal or one of a larger size? A good journal gives you plenty of room to write and is something you will be able to carry easily so you can capture those great ideas that come up during the day. Some people prefer to use a software journaling program, such as the one found at www.life-journal.com. If that works best for you, go for it but you'll want a way to record those *thoughts as you are on the go.* Your journal should be sacred and always available for your thoughts, ideas, insights, frustrations, and victories. Re-reading your entries over time will accelerate your evolution as a coach and the growth of your business possibilities and opportunities. The key point is finding what feels right for you and is functional so that you use it!!!

We have a pretty clear picture of what you *don't* want in your career. You listed these points earlier and we shared comments from some of our participants and clients. Be sure to write these in your journal. Shifting from what isn't working to a new, more functional and fitting model is not an alien concept but, surprisingly, therapists often fail to apply it to themselves. When we ask therapists to tell us what they do want in their careers, the responses are interesting.

> Hmmmm. . . . Gee, I don't know. I guess I want more money, less work, more prestige, and a lot more fun.

> I want more time to enjoy my life. I want exercise and balance and time to write. I want to enjoy my children and be home when they get home from school.

> I want to be true to my values in working with my clients. I feel managed care has forced me into a bind between doing what I believe is right for my clients and doing what they will pay for.
>
> I'm doubting my abilities and myself. I want to feel strong, positive and capable as a helper.

> It seems I'm clearer about what I don't want than what I do want. There has to be something more than this, a better way of doing the helping work that is challenging, fun, makes a difference, and also gives me energy rather than drains me on a daily basis.

TRY IT!

What do I want for my practice? This is a very important question for your transition journey. What do you want? Really want? Really, really, really want? Deb often leads coaching workshop participants through a focused visualization exercise where they identify and list some of the wants they have in major categories of their lives.

In your journal, write what you want in answer to the questions below. Deb has offered a list of wants from herself and clients as examples to help you see how we write them. The more specific you are, the more likely you are to get what you really want.

Find a quiet place where you can think uninterrupted about your life. What do you *have* in your life that you want more of? What is

(continued on next page)

something you *don't* have that you'd like added to your life? What do you *have* or *do* that you'd like to change or eliminate? What have you dreamed about or always wanted to *do* but just haven't taken steps toward for whatever reason? Think about the person you are and what you really value in your life. What would you do to *be* different in your life? Here are some examples of written wants from Deb and some of her clients. Notice the pattern of the want statements.

I want daily reflection and journaling time in my schedule.
I want a simplified record-keeping process for my finances.
I want to take on only work that feels like play.
I want to travel with my husband for a month in New Zealand.
I want my children and grandchildren to have the lives of their
    dreams.
I want to eat only nutritious foods and to exercise on a daily basis.
I want to develop deep soulful relationships with special people
    in my life.
I want to retire at 50.
I want to spend more time with my family.
I want to get a massage.
I want to wear only clothes that feel like pajamas
I want to celebrate daily my wonderful life and many blessings.

The great thing about wants is that they are freely exchanged. If you see a want on the above list that applies to you, write it on your list. In workshops we freely exchange wants and this helps all of us think more creatively.

So, following the above pattern of I want _____, answer the following questions for yourself. Write your want statements in your journal. One per line. Write whatever (*having, doing,* or *being*) that comes up after reading the question, as many as you can think of.

In the life area of *relationships,* what do you want?
In the life area of *leisure,* what do you want?
When you think about your *finances,* what do you want?
What to you want in the area of *health* and *wellness?*

(continued on next page)

When you think about what you want for your *family members,*
   what do you discover?
What do you want in the life area of your *work* or your *career*?
What do you want in the life area of *spirituality*?
When you think about making a *difference in your world* or being
   of *service,* what do you want?
When you think about the area of *travel,* what do you want?
Want do you want in the area of your *continuing education*?
What have you been dreaming about that you *really, really, really*
   want?

Spend some time recording your wants. After writing all you can,
come up with two to three really significant wants in each life area that
you'd like to work on achieving. Contemplate these wants as you continue your journey. Write them each on a 3 x 5 card and place them
someplace so that you will see them every day—such as on your bath-
room mirror, your car steering wheel, your computer monitor. If the
wants are truly important, you will use them to guide your actions as
you develop your life coaching practice. Make a plan today to start
getting what you want in your life.

Do You Have What It Takes?

We have already told you we believe that therapists are eminently qualified
to be life coaches. You are well educated and well trained; you possess the
necessary critical helping skills; you have many skills and talents—all of
these are essential ingredients for successful life coaches. If we asked you to
write your qualifications in your journal, you could come up with a long list.
Other than additional training specific to life coaching, you are ready to start
today. So, what is holding you back?

During our experience coaching and training hundreds of therapists
during the past several years, we have discovered what we believe to be the
most important ingredient for a successful transition from therapist to life
coach. It isn't where you went to college or how you were trained as a therapist; it isn't how successful your therapy practice has been or even how
many years you have been a helping professional. The most important indi-
cator of success in transitioning from therapist to life coach is *your ability to
make a change.* Plain and simple.

We have seen relatively new therapists transition smoothly into a full-time life coaching practice in a short time while other experienced professionals struggle to infuse coaching into their practices on even a part-time basis. This journey will require you to think and act differently as a helping professional. We'll discuss some of these differences more specifically later. We understand it is scary to let go of the way you have always worked and try something new. This is plain old fear, a common emotion for individuals facing any transition. Whether you are planning to close your therapy practice completely and jump head first into life coaching or whether you want to stick your toes in first and try it on a part-time basis, there is often some fear associated.

As we tell our therapy clients, these fears are likely based on our negative beliefs about the world or ourselves. If you hold on to these fears, you won't be able to take the risks, seize the opportunities, and develop the positive perspective necessary to function successfully as a life coach. Common fears many therapists share are the fear of marketing themselves as life coaches, of managing their coaching practices as businesses. You may share these fears or have others that occur to you as you read this chapter. You can recognize them as the little voices in the back of your head trying to persuade you to put this book down and go back to doing what you know how to do, therapy. Stay with these thoughts and feelings a little longer and record them in your journal.

TRY IT!

As you try to see yourself developing a new practice as a life coach, what negative beliefs or fears stand in your way? Make a list of these in your journal. Put an asterisk by the ones that seem most powerful. Here are a few we have gathered from our clients and ourselves:

I'll go broke!
I can't market myself!
I can't run a business!
No one is going to pay me to do this!
I'm throwing away an expensive education and a lot of training!

It has been our experience that, in time, as you learn more about life coaching and have some successes, the fears subside and you are ready to go for what you really want. Find support, try new things, and see yourself in a new light. All we ask is for you to be a willing, active, and involved participant.

TRY IT!

Give yourself at least an hour for this exercise. Write your life story in your journal. How did you come to this point in your personal and professional world?

Total Life Design

If you are going to be a credible coach, live your life as you coach others to live theirs. This does not mean *your* life has to be *perfect*. Living purposefully means living in full awareness of what can be improved in your life and what you want to maintain or eliminate. This is why we believe it is essential that you also have a personal coach, especially in the beginning of your transition. Even later, when you are successful, having your own coach keeps you focused on what really matters, and aware of how your clients may experience the process of coaching. We both have had coaches throughout our transitions and hire specialists from time to time.

Much of our approach is presented as Total Life Coaching™. We believe that Total Life Coaching is the operating system for all coaching, whether it is business coaching, executive or corporate coaching, or personal coaching. As the operating system, it is always in the background of all coaching conversations. For example, a client may be focused on career-specific coaching, but as a coach you can also bring up ways to at least look at other areas of his or her life that may benefit from some attention. We use a Life Balance Wheel or coaching mandala (included in the welcome packet found at the back of the book) as a system for exploring clients' main life areas and to help them learn that a balanced life most often leads to a successful manifestation of what it is that they want to accomplish in any one area of their life. Later, you will have an opportunity to work with the coaching mandala.

Living Your Life on Purpose

Truly effective coaching unleashes the individual spirit and deep desires, expands the client's capacity to achieve real change, and perhaps even provides personal transformation. This does not occur with simple techniques like goal setting and motivation. It occurs when coaching considers the underlying context for change and alters the client's experience of living more *on purpose*. If you are going to be an effective coach, in a whole-person context, then we believe it is essential for you to also have done the work. Most coach training programs teach a variety of techniques and strategies for coaching but many are about external skills. To be a truly masterful coach, you also must work on changing from within because the profession of coaching is more about your *beingness* than skills or techniques.

Many of us have experienced psychotherapy as patients, perhaps as an educational requirement or because we had our own healing work to complete. Similarly we believe that masterful coaches must experience coaching on a regular basis and work with a coach on the very issues or desires that your clients will also benefit from. For us, that starts with looking at one's life purpose, or life design.

Clients will indeed come to coaching for more mundane reasons than designing their life, but whatever the presenting objectives, there is always the possibility of introducing the concept of Total Life Coaching™. For that process you, as the coach, must have experienced the power of designing your life and living more *on purpose*. You will have an opportunity to explore your life purpose in a future exercise.

Some coaching schools call this concept "coaching from the inside out." We consider it part of a coach's total life design but, whatever you call it, we believe that it will help you discover ways to coach your clients about life design and personal fulfillment. In the process, this concept will be useful and perhaps transformational for you as well. Being able to "walk the talk" as a coach means that you have experienced what you suggest for your clients and that you implement the skills so that your life is a model for your clients. Again, this does not mean that you are living the life of a saint or that you are some enlightened master; it means that you live your life purposefully and are aware when you *get in your own way*. You must be committed to modeling how it is to be living a fulfilling life or be on the path to creating a fulfilling life. You will generally attract clients who are one step behind or one step ahead of where you are. Remember, sometimes the student is also the teacher.

Coaching As an Interdevelopmental Process

As you work on living your life more authentically, you will also come to find that much of the joyfulness of the coaching profession is that both you and the client evolve in the coaching process. For you to model a great life, you should be living a great life or at least moving rapidly on that path. Your life cannot be a mess if your coaching business is going to thrive or if your coaching is to be truly effective. Your personal transformation will provide more practical magic for your clients.

TRY IT!

Using the Life Balance Wheel (figure 3.1) give yourself a score from 1–10 in each of the life areas. Which ones show the biggest gap between where you are now and where you want to be? Identify and record in your journal what you want to do to make the scores higher (to at least an 8). Now, who can help you work on closing these gaps? Do you have a coach or a buddy, or can you work on this yourself? We recommend you work with your own coach, as this is exactly where you will also start with your clients. Write in your journal what you discovered during this exercise and identify three actions you will take in the next week to help you narrow the gaps and achieve what you want.

Figure 3.1. **Life Balance Wheel (Coaching Mandala)**

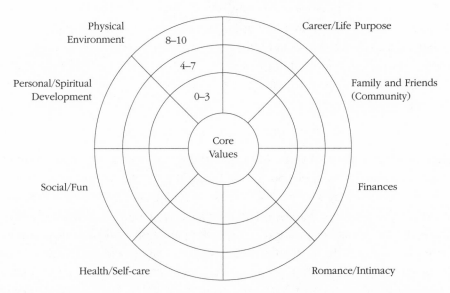

© Patrick Williams, Institute for Life Coach Training

The hub represents your core values—each area interrelated in an ideal life. Give yourself a score (1–10) and shade or color in the space accordingly. Use this coaching mandala as a way to assess the level of life satisfaction in each area. You may score it numerically to measure the improvement desired, or you may use it to have a coaching conversation about gaps between where you are now and where you would like to be.

We are going to provide a taste of the total life coaching concept. The purpose of this chapter is not to give you all the methods for this total life-design work that is available in our formal coach training program through the Institute for Life Coach Training. However, we will give you the key starting point for your journey into coaching.

De-cluttering Your Life

After completing your Life Balance Wheel assessment, the next place to start is to look at what gets in your way of having a great life. We call this process "de-cluttering" because it invariably involves the actual tossing and cleaning up of clutter like boxes of books, pictures, files, etc.—all the stuff that clutters our closets, our garages, our offices, and our lives. Believe us when we say that getting rid of physical clutter actually helps you gain energy in your life. There is a part of you connected to all your stuff and the more organized and uncluttered your physical space is, the more room you have for what you really want.

This is equally true for the nonphysical clutter in your life. Emotional baggage that still needs unpacking; important conversations that are needed in significant relationships; handling concerns about money, your body, etc. These are not necessarily therapy issues. They are just psychological clutter that needs work. This is a great area to work on with a mentor coach.

Energy Drainers and Energy Gainers

Cheryl Richardson speaks of eliminating things that drain you and replacing them with things that fuel you in her book *Take Time for Your Life*. This is common terminology and practice in the coaching field. Energy drainers are those things (activities, habits, relationships, or clutter) that cost you energy. These are the items on your to-do list, procrastinations, piles of files, or anything else that you have not finished dong or dealing with. As each item is taken care of, you reclaim the energy that was attached to it. Then you have more energy to focus on what really matters. You can have more *choice* in your life. In fact, we believe that *depression* is actually *depletion* and as one replenishes oneself by eliminating energy drainers and choosing more energy gainers, they will be less depleted (and less depressed). Our friend and fellow coach Philip Humbert calls this work "personal ecology."

TRY IT!

THE FIRST STEP OF DE-CLUTTERING

Using the form on the following page, make a list of what you are putting up with at work and at home to determine what energy drainers might be limiting you right now. Now is the time to identify those things. As you think of more items, add them to your list. You may or may not choose to do anything about them right now, but just becoming aware of and articulating them will bring them to the forefront where you'll naturally start eliminating, fixing, or resolving them.

For example, look at your office. Your office is the seat of your coaching business and creating space there is the first step toward creating space in your life for your coaching business. Is there clutter? Disorganization? Is it set up in such a way as to give you energy? Does your office make you feel peaceful and comfortable? Make your working space perfect for you, even if you work at home. You must have the physical space, the time space, and the emotional space for you to transition to *being* a coach. Other places to look for energy drainers are in relationships that have what Fritz Perls (1973) used to call "unfinished business." You might need to have what we call a "courageous conversation" to clean up some part of the relationship. You will regain energy when you do. You can also look at your to-do list and other things you have wanted to work on. Make it a priority to take care of all the things on this list by focusing and committing. Coaching wisdom is to follow this edict: Do it, dump it, or delegate it. Look at the tasks at hand and the things you are putting up with, follow that wisdom, and get complete.

ENERGY DRAINERS AT WORK	ENERGY DRAINERS AT HOME
1.	1.
2.	2.
3.	3.
4.	4.
5.	5.
6.	6.
7.	7.
8.	8.
9.	9.
10.	10.

(continued on next page)

Now, after you have experienced great relief in whittling down your list of energy drainers, it is important to go the extra step and choose consciously to have energy gainers in your life. These may fall in the realm of positive daily or weekly habits, like exercise, meditation, or time with friends, family, and your spouse or life partner. Energy gainers are those things or activities that give you a charge of joy, fun, passion, or peace and comfort. We often have these in our life, but they get pushed aside by the energy drainers. As you take care of your energy drainers, you now have time to choose energy gainers purposefully.

THE SECOND STEP OF DE-CLUTTERING
(Charging the Batteries)

Make a list of those things that impact your life in a positive way. They can be things you do (or want to do more of), people you like to be around, favorite aspects of your physical environment (artwork, music, an organized living or work space).

At work one client that we know gets energy from having a stereo in her office and a supply of soothing CDs; another gets energy from a daily jog with colleagues in her work area; another loves to help coordinate a biweekly potluck for her office staff. At home, one client has a daily journaling ritual with a special place to sit with fragrant candles; another schedules a weekly lunch out with a friend where they always have a healthy and nutritious meal; a third schedules a massage in his hotel room when he is traveling away from home. Make a list below of some energy gainers you'd like to bring into your life.

ENERGY GAINERS AT WORK	ENERGY GAINERS AT HOME
1.	1.
2.	2.
3.	3.
4.	4.
5.	5.
6.	6.
7.	7.
8.	8.
9.	9.
10.	10.

Strengthening Your Personal Integrity

A big part of your work as a coach is living with a high degree of *personal integrity*. What do we mean? In engineering, integrity has to do with the foundation of the structure. The integrity of a bridge or skyscraper is in its strong foundation and structure that insures the safety and functionality of the final creation. We are no different. For the *design, creation,* and *structure* of our lives to be the best it can be, we must have a strong personal integrity or foundational congruence. In other words, we are out of integrity if our underlying foundation is weak and we are not able to stand tall and firm in the life we want to live.

Having integrity as a coach means doing what it takes to make your vision of a fulfilling, purposeful life a reality. Much of the work here is aligning your values with your purpose and vision for your ideal life, and then finding ways for them to be a reality and not just wishes. Much of this is part of a good coach training program that emphasizes the importance of personal transformation work for successful life coaching. It is beyond the scope of this book to present this detailed training but we will reference training and or reading throughout our book that we believe will further enhance your personal integrity. This is another perfect opportunity to work with a mentor coach.

Finding Yourself and Renewing your Soul

We believe that we are even better helping professionals as life coaches than as therapists. Time and again we hear the same response from therapists who have made the transition. Here's what Carole Kunkle-Miller, one of our graduates and a former full-time therapist, has to share:

> I was skeptical as to whether I could really make the transition from full-time psychologist to coach. I moved slowly at first, probably due to my fears about giving up the known versus the unknown. I have now learned to think about myself and my gifts in a big way, much different than I had ever thought of myself before. I now have a popular e-zine, an interview with *Working Woman* magazine, an interview with National Public Radio, and my coaching clients are quickly growing. Managed care is not totally out of my picture yet, but imagine my excitement to write

a letter of resignation to one of the big companies this week. I don't need them anymore. What a wonderful transformation!!!

You are not alone on this journey. We will help coach you through this transition as you participate in activities and explorations. We will provide rich resources carefully designed to help in finding yourself and renewing your soul as a helping professional. You will also be joined in spirit by the words of both therapists who have made the transition and participants in the Institute for Life Coach Training program. As you begin to realize that it is the quality of your efforts that matters, failure becomes unthinkable. How can you fail to become yourself? Are you ready to begin? Do you have what it takes?

PART II

Life Coaching for Therapists

CHAPTER FOUR

Therapy and Coaching: Distinctions and Similarities

If you want to change attitudes, start with a change in behavior.

—William Glasser

The ability to change is a premier prerequisite for making a successful transition from therapy into life coaching and we recognize that change takes courage. We hope that you are excited about the opportunities life coaching offers for helpers and clients and that you are ready to proceed learning more of the nitty-gritty.

Beyond the ability to change, our research indicates two additional traits you'll want to develop to have a successful coaching practice:

1. Understand the distinctions between therapy and coaching
2. Develop the business and entrepreneurial skills necessary to build a successful coaching practice

We'll detail business and entrepreneurial skills later in the book. For now, let's examine, first, distinctions, then similarities of coaching and therapy.

Distinctions Between Therapy and Coaching

As the profession of life coaching evolves, it becomes more uniquely defined and described. Over the past several years we've seen increasing clarity of its role and definition (Barlow, 1998; Ellis, 1998; Menendez & Lowry, 1997; Steele, 1999; Williams, 2000a); these distinctions continue to emerge even as you read this book. Increasingly, we believe that life coaching is an evolutionary step beyond traditional therapy. We don't believe traditional therapy will become extinct but will be more associated with the clients who need clinical services. On a continuum, it might look something like this:

Traditional Therapy— (old style)	Transitional Models— (gray areas)	Coaching— (a new option)
Psychoanalytic	Solution-focused brief	Whole life coaching
Paradigm of pathology	Paradigm of solutions	Paradigm of possibility
Orientation		Orientation
Process		Outcome
Feelings		Action
Inner world		Inner to outer worlds
History	Language is primary tool	Vision of Future
"Why?"		"How?"
Therapist is expert	Move away from pathology	Therapist as cocreator
Client is patient		Partnership of equals
Medical model		Freedom from managed care

Like how some of the traditional models blended into the more solution-focused perspectives and clients moved between both, we believe cross referrals will occur between solution-focused therapists and coaches as the public becomes clearer about the appropriateness of each profession. Several leaders in the solution-focused movement such as Insoo Kim Berg (1994) and Steve de Shazer (1985) use powerful language and possibility thinking strategies, which are very useful for therapists transitioning into life coaching. The distinctions between the solution-focused therapies and coaching are not as simple to delineate as they blend more than with the traditional, more analytic, models of therapy. Again, we believe it is an evolution of the helping profession which will eventually help clients more clearly determine the helping professional who is the "best fit" for their current concern. Figure 4.1 illustrates our thinking.

Figure 4.1. **Therapy and Coaching in Relationship**

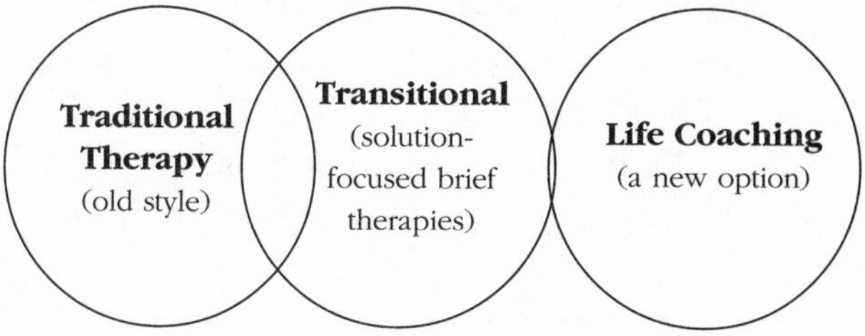

We would like to consider the distinctions between traditional therapy and coaching in four broad categories.

1. *Past vs. future: Perspectives on the process.* Therapy focuses on the *past* and generally assumes the client has a problem that needs solving; coaching focuses on the *future* and assumes the client is whole and capable of having a wonderful life.
2. *Fix vs. create: Why clients come to see you.* Clients seek a therapist as a source of *fixing* or eliminating their problem; clients seek a coach to help them get *more* out of their lives or *create* new possibilities in their lives.
3. *Professional vs. collegial: Characteristics of the helper-client relationship.* Therapy clients see the therapist as an *expert* who holds the answers and techniques to fix their problems; coaching clients see the coach as a *partner* to support their growth and efforts to create an even better life than they have now.
4. *Limited vs. open: How you generate new clients.* Therapists are *limited* in the ways they can generate clients and how readily they can approach others about their services; coaches can be *free* and open about seeking clients and discussing their services.

We'll look at each of these distinction categories individually and then move on to how therapy and coaching are similar.

Past versus Future: Perspectives on the Process

From our perspective, therapy has historically dealt with the client's past and some pain or dysfunction. The helper's role was to bring the client to an adequate present or reasonable level of functioning (taking the dysfunction into consideration). Coaching, by contrast, is working with an individual who is already adequately functioning and moving with him to a higher level of functioning.* Imagine you are driving your car down the freeway. If you look in the rearview mirror toward where you have been, you look at the past— that is therapy. If you look out the front windshield toward where you are going and the road beyond your vision, you look toward the future—that is life coaching.

Now, we know some of you reading this are saying, "But I work in the future when I do therapy!" and this may well be the case, particularly if you are trained and practice from a solution-focused perspective. However, we would suggest that if you are helping adequately functioning individuals move to higher levels of functioning by using coaching techniques, you probably aren't doing therapy or, at least, therapy as defined by most insurance companies. We recognize there are some coachlike therapists. In fact, they are usually the individuals most comfortable with the therapist-coach transition.

We know traditional psychotherapy focused on the root of the problem, the history, the family of origin, the everything of origin! Coaching, from a theoretical perspective, focuses on the future, barrier identification, goal setting, planning, and creative action. Coaching works with the conscious mind actively in order to facilitate the client to step into a preferred future while also living a fulfilling life in the present.

Fix versus Create: Why Clients Come to See You

In most clinical practices, clients come with a presenting problem either that they want you to solve or because someone else has sent them to see you so you will "fix" them. We see a lot of the latter in marital therapy.

If you apply the traditional medical model of therapy, you'd undertake strategies similar to the following: First, you would talk with the client about her personal and medical histories, and previous mental health treatment. You would explore the history and duration of the problem. You would talk with the client about why she believes she might have this problem at this time in her life and continue to gather pertinent current and historical infor-

---

*While it is not the focus of this book, we'd like to note that there are coaches who have specialties working with people who might not fall into the category of "adequately functioning." For example, there are specialized coaches who work within a school system with disturbed youth who are also in therapy.

mation. Next, you would get out your *DSM-IV* and, based on all the history and information you have gathered, you give the client a diagnosis and develop a treatment plan.

Now, if the client has insurance, the diagnosis is hopefully one that the insurance company will accept. If not, then you face the common dilemma of deciding whether you will assign a *DSM-IV* diagnosis that would enable the client to get insurance reimbursement. Many therapists face this decision on a daily basis and often will assign a *DSM* diagnosis simply to enable the client to get reimbursement, not because the diagnosis is helpful in any way. This is the sad reality of managed care and the medical model in the helping professions.

Beyond the above dilemma, we must consider the client's perspective throughout this relationship. Clients assume that they will be "fixed" and have emotional healing as a result of their relationship with a therapist because that is why they wanted therapy in the first place.

Coaching clients, on the other hand, come to see you for a myriad of reasons but most of them relate to their future. Often they've heard of you from a friend or colleague who also has a life coach and is doing great things with their life. They usually do not come because they have a major problem, certainly not a major psychological one. They are not coming with a dysfunction. Typically they are not coming in pain. They might have a little general malaise because they are wanting more out of their lives and don't know how to get it. They don't need, or usually even desire, a diagnostic label. They don't have something broken that needs an expert to "fix." They just want something more out of their lives (work, relationships, career, spiritual practice, physical wellness, etc.). The assumption is that by working with you they will have greater success in planning, setting goals, and creating the lives of their dreams. Coaching is not about *fixing;* coaching is about *creating.*

If a client with a major psychological problem comes to see you (in your life coaching practice) the appropriate action is to refer that client to a qualified therapist. Our coach training program curriculum speaks to this area in depth and further addresses the nuances for professionals who want to maintain *both* a therapy and a coaching practice. As a general rule of practice, we believe you should keep *miles* between your coaching and therapy practices if you choose to have both. Additionally, we believe that once a person has been your coaching client, you should not take them into your therapy practice. The reverse is mostly true, but a therapist may do coaching with a former therapy client as long as there is a ritual ending of the therapy relationship, and the new coaching relationship is begun formally and clearly. The majority of our graduates leave therapy for a complete transition into coaching and maintain a list of qualified therapists for referrals. Likewise, we know therapists who refer clients to life coaches when the client has resolved their therapeutic issues and is ready to move forward with their life design and plans.

Professional versus Collegial: Characteristics of the Helper-Client Relationship

In the therapeutic relationship, the therapist is often assumed to be the "expert" and sometimes therapists feel that clients expect them to know the solution to their problems. The power, at least from the client's view, typically rests with the therapist. This is one of the reasons why we spend so much time in our therapeutic training learning about boundaries, ethical standards, transference, and all the other issues revolving around the "counselor-patient" relationship. Again, we understand that some of you do all you can to assure your clients keep their power in your therapeutic practice, however, you must admit that when you get down to the nitty-gritty, you, the therapist, are guiding the counseling process. You are the "professional" and hold a great deal of power in the relationship, whether you want it or not.

Active Partnership

By contrast, the coaching relationship is very equal, more like an active partnership. A successful life coaching relationship is collegial and balanced. Life coaches recognize that clients really have the knowledge and the solutions; the coach simply helps unlock their brilliance. Consider this dialog difference between therapy and coaching clients.

THERAPY CLIENT: "I just don't know what is the matter with me, I'm so depressed."

COACHING CLIENT: "I'm not sure where to go next; I want to have more time with my family but I'm just not sure how to make it work and keep this job."

Coaching clients often know where they want to go, coaches help them clarify their goals and see their way more clearly. There is not a power differential per se in coaching. Good coaches make a conscious effort to keep the relationship balanced. Again, we recognize that some of you conduct your therapeutic sessions more like the life coaching sessions we described than traditional therapy. That's great, because you are that much closer to practicing successfully as a life coach!

If you were to observe a coaching session, you would see that it is typically very open, often friendly, casual, and light. Life coaches laugh with their clients and, when appropriate, may even joke or gently tease. With caution, life coaches may feel comfortable sharing their personal experiences that are pertinent to what the client is experiencing. Clients and coaches feel like they really know each other on a deeper level than possibly many other professional relationships. Many coaching clients report that they appreciate that openness.

We want to be very clear here that we believe coaches are professionals and should act accordingly. We endorse the International Coach Federation Code of Ethics (see the resources) and train from a model of high standards of professional behavior. The difference we are addressing is the relationship between the coach and the client and how each perceives the other and their relationship.

Public Contact

Another second difference between coaching and therapeutic relationships is how you handle public contact with your client. Yes, you do maintain confidentiality and, unless your client gives permission, you do not automatically disclose they are clients. This is something you discuss up front with the client during the intake interview that we will discuss further in chapter 7. Most coaching clients readily offer permission for disclosure and the level of openness is far greater than typically permitted in a therapeutic relationship. For example, you can even talk to them in the grocery store. Here is Deb's story:

> When I was practicing in a small town in rural southcentral Alaska, I always felt awkward seeing my therapy clients at the mall or grocery store because I was so conscious of confidentiality concerns. In no way did I want to violate their right to privacy or let

on that they were seeing me to others who clearly knew my work. It was always a dance as to whether to acknowledge them or not and when I didn't, I felt uncomfortable even though we'd discussed confidentiality in therapy and how that translated to the real world.

Sometimes they'd say, 'Hi Dr. Deb' and my young daughter would say, 'How do you know them?' and I'd say, 'Uh . . . from work' . . . and she'd say, 'Oh, I get it.' Now, as a coach, when I meet a client we often hug and share warm greetings. Frequently, clients introduce me to friends or family members by saying, 'Hey, here's Deb, she's my coach.' Typically the friend responds with, 'Yeah? What sport?' and we are off on the path of defining and clarifying life coaching.

Coaching clients appreciate not having the stigma attached to life coaching that can still unfortunately accompany therapy. While society is changing, coaching clients are much more likely to tell others that they are seeing or talking to a life coach than they would be disclosing they are going to a therapist.

How, When, and Where We Meet Clients

Life coaching can occur in a variety of formats. The options are numerous with regard to location and time frames. You might meet your client in a coffeehouse, your office, an airport club lounge, or exclusively on the telephone. Likewise you could meet for half an hour, an hour, or a full day. Many coaches meet with their clients for one-to-two-day sessions, usually once a year or perhaps in the beginning of the relationship. Due to the time and cost, this is usually for the executive or business owner who can afford such time. During these intensive coaching sessions, the coach usually explores all life areas in more depth with the client and they cocreate detailed action plans and identify ways to address obstacles. They may develop a clearer vision and mission, both professional and personally, and create a Total Life Plan, designing the focus and intentions for many months and years ahead. These "intensives" are a powerful way to create a strong relationship between coach and client and an investment by the client in transformational goals for their life and work.

It is important that you remember to remain flexible, explore multiple delivery approaches, and be guided by client's needs and wants. We encourage therapist-trained coaches to consider the variety of potential coaching formats for clients and not assume that a face-to-face 50-minute hour of therapy is necessarily the best fit for all life coaching clients.

A life coaching session can occur anywhere that makes sense for the client and the coach. The majority of our current life coaching clients meet with us via the telephone. We also have had face-to-face clients and believe in using multiple contact sources for clients, including letters, faxes, or e-mail in addition to our regular coaching phone calls.

Often therapist-trained coaches are concerned about using formats other than a face-to-face one. After years of studying and practicing the important aspects of body language (nonverbal behavior, proximity, office arrangement, etc.), it is difficult to imagine a successful helping relationship in any other format. However, we assure you, life coaching over the telephone is a very viable format for this particular helping relationship.

We have been asked if there is a qualitative difference between face-to-face life coaching and coaching over the telephone. Our sense is that it depends on the topic and the client. For most situations, the telephone medium works great. For some clients, it is anonymous so they disclose more than they might in person. Coaching over the telephone also works great for busy adults. They can simply close their office door and pick up the telephone for their coaching call instead of having to drive to a life coach's office or other meeting place. Working over the phone also allows the life coach to take detailed notes, consult resources, and stay focused on what the client is saying without the distractions of nonverbal behaviors and appearance. By contrast, some clients, at first, feel more comfortable meeting with their coach in person and are more open to sharing their life dreams in the coach's presence. The bottom line is what works best for each client and the level of flexibility you are willing to establish in your practice.

Here are some tips for therapists transitioning to telephone coaching:

1. Take some telecourse coach training courses. These experiences will boost your confidence regarding what you can accomplish over the telephone.
2. Buy the best equipment you can afford. A quality headset is worth every penny you expend for comfort, audio clarity, and the feeling of connectedness with your client.
3. Start slowly. If you have some in-person clients, try coaching them on the phone when they are traveling or call them at their office for a change of

pace. If you plan only telephone clients, start with a couple and build up. You will quickly learn to love this medium of communication.

4. Plan to eliminate distractions just as you would if you were with the client in person. Stay focused on the client. Just because he or she can't see you, avoid opening your mail, working on your computer, or playing with your dog.

5. Make an agreement with your client to report when either of you has difficulty hearing during your call. This removes the anxiety that maybe you aren't picking up all the details of the conversation.

Similar to *where* life coaches meet their clients, *when* and *how long* they meet them depends in large part on the needs of the client and the coach. Some coaches prefer a structured format, such as a monthly retainer and weekly half-hour phone calls. However, this is only one format. Other coaches find this much too short a coaching session and prefer an hour and fifteen minutes or anything in between. Some coaches schedule daily ten-minute telephone check-ins when they are helping clients with specific habit changes. Face-to-face coaching sessions can span hours, days, or even minutes. The options are limitless.

This difference between therapy and coaching provides a whole new sense of openness and opportunity. It permits you to travel and still maintain your schedule or to have international clients and develop a schedule that accommodates both of your needs. The key ingredients are creativity and flexibility. You can create any system that serves your clients and works for you and you can also change it over time to everyone's best advantage.

That leads us right into the next distinction between therapy and coaching—how you get your clients.

Limited versus Open: How You Generate New Clients

The traditional therapist finds new clients through referral sources and possible advertisements in the yellow pages. Therapists with a more entrepreneurial inclination may generate clients through presentations in the community, teaching a college class, or even by having a Web page. However, as therapists seeking new clients, we generally rely on pretty soft approaches and we often don't market ourselves in the traditional sense. For example, if someone starts to disclose a personal concern at a dinner party, we typically wouldn't say, "Oh, I'd love to be your therapist, I believe I can really help you resolve that problem." But as a coach, the situation changes.

When you get into the same conversation as a life coach, it would be very appropriate to say, "Well, I'd love to coach you on that. I believe you can figure that one out pretty quickly. If you are interested, we can give it a try. Why don't you call me up for a complimentary session and we can work on it? Here's my business card." This is not pushy, it is just offering your service to someone who looks like a great new client. It is perfectly ethical and, in fact, is the right thing to do if you really believe you can support the individual in reaching his or her life dreams and you have room in your practice. It's still a mode of attraction to get clients, but you can say more and go further as a life coach than you can as a therapist trying to gain new therapy clients. In fact, good coaches could ask someone who has described a challenge or life obstacle if they would be interested in being coached, right then, for a few minutes on that issue. This powerful interaction demonstrates immediately what life coaching is about rather than trying to find the appropriate words to describe it.

Similarities between Therapy and Coaching

Now that we have discussed the differences between therapy and coaching, let's examine some of the transferable skills we believe good therapists bring to the life coaching relationship. Your academic preparation and training as a helping professional whether as a counselor, social worker, family therapist, psychiatrist, or psychologist is highly applicable and relevant to the coaching relationship. It is in this area where therapy and coaching are most similar. Over the past 20 years, some schools of therapy have begun to look more like coaching programs. In fact, some universities now offer coaching classes as part of their counseling curricula. We also know doctoral students who are doing their dissertations on coaching principles. These events will continue to provide us with enhanced information about the coaching relationship.

Depending on what kind of background you have, much of what you've learned as a therapist will serve you well as a life coach. Listening skills, reframing, positive regard for the client, note taking and process skills are just a few transferable skills. Additionally, you know how to conduct intake interviews, discuss difficult issues with clients, and have probably heard such a variety of stories in therapy that you won't be surprised with the issues that come to coaching. If you are trained in solution-focused therapy, which uses a group of questions to focus the client's attention and awareness on what works rather than what is broken, you already have a valuable set of tools you can transfer to life coaching.

TRY IT!

Consider the major therapeutic approaches listed below. In your journal, make a list of the skills, techniques, and strategies you've developed as a therapist that you believe would be valuable in the coaching relationship.

Psychodynamic	Gestalt therapy
Rogerian/Humanistic	Solution-focused therapy
Cognitive-behavioral	Ericksonian
Behavioral	Neuro-linguistic programming
Developmental	Psychosynthesis
Family systems therapy	Add others with which you are familiar
Group therapy	

For example, you may have learned from cognitive therapy that it is important to separate thought from emotion. From Ericksonian approaches you may have learned reframing and your Rogerian training may have taught you the value of unconditional positive regard. All of these are valuable skills to retain for your life coaching practice.

We hope you identified some overlaps between your preparation as a trained helping professional and your work as a life coach. There are some additional similarities between therapy and coaching that extend beyond the transferable skills you, as a trained helping professional, bring to the relationship.

SHARED CHARACTERISTICS OF THERAPY AND COACHING

These include, but are not limited to:

A fee is paid for the service.
The client wants to change.
You are in a professional helper role.

(continued on next page)

It is an ongoing, confidential, typically one-to-one relationship.

The dialogue between you and the client is a primary vehicle for delivering the service.

Listening is perhaps the most critical skill upon which your success depends.

The relationship can be group-based.

The sessions are regularly scheduled.

There is an assumption that change occurs over a period of time.

TRY IT!

This is an exercise we often do with therapists who transition to life coaching. We believe it is very important to examine and be upfront about the assumptions you currently hold about clients and the helping relationship. These come from years of education, training, and practice.

Step 1. Ask yourself the following question: "What are some of the key assumptions I've developed as a therapist about the following topics?" Use your journal to record your responses.

1. The therapeutic relationship.
2. The clients I see.
3. The way I get clients.

Step 2. Thinking about some of the distinctions between therapy and life coaching we've discussed in this chapter, review what you just wrote and ask yourself, "What are some of the assumptions I've made about myself and my role as a helper that I need to examine because they may not fit for coaching?"

For example, another common therapeutic assumption is that something is wrong or broken and needs "fixing" in the client's life. Coaches do not make this assumption but assume the client is whole and not in need of repair.

Step 3. Take time to examine and record your assumptions and what you discovered about them in your journal. Here's an example: "I discovered that I often feel pressure to be the *expert* in the helping relationship. I always feel like I should know the answer and the client is looking to me for the solutions. I don't like this feeling because much of the time I really believe the client knows better than I where they should go from here."

When Deb teaches workshops, she often describes changing our therapeutic assumptions to the coaching perspective as analogous to resetting the default buttons on your computer. In therapy, we've been trained to function from a certain operating system. As you begin to transition into the coaching perspective, and operate from coaching assumptions, it is necessary to reset the default buttons on your own internal operating system so that you can think and act like a coach rather than as a therapist.

In summary, the coaching profession is evolving and we are continually developing increasing awareness of the distinctions and similarities between therapy and coaching. Therapists are learning that we have many transferable skills and appropriate preparation that serve us well as we transition from helping professionals to life coaches. However, we are also recognizing that the two relationships are distinctive and some of the assumptions we've made as therapists are not appropriate in the life coaching relationship. It is your obligation as a professional wanting to be a great life coach to recognize and modify or eliminate the assumptions and practices that may stand in the way of success for your coaching clients.

How to Make the Distinctions Work

Some of you may have discovered that the education and training you've received have led you to develop strong therapeutic assumptions and practices significantly different from what will best serve you in life coaching. You will need to consciously reframe, drop some traditional behaviors, and learn some new ones.

For others, the shift will not seem so great. Consider this comment from Roz Van Meter, one of our workshop participants and a graduate of the Institute for Life Coach Training:

> With regard to the transition from therapist to coach, for some of us, the step is small. The transition is really not tough. Those of us who have been doing Gestalt-type "how" rather than "why" therapy for years and who are very outcome oriented in their counseling and not stuck in the medical model negotiate this transition swiftly. Especially if we are accustomed to working for fees only. We find no trouble distinguishing between therapy and coaching because we've been doing coaching for years in our offices and just calling it therapy.

What is most important is that you recognize the differences between therapy and coaching, understand and acknowledge your assumptions that may interfere with the life coaching relationship, and take action to minimize and eliminate any potential interference. Here are some suggestions to help you make the distinctions work.

Do not use the "why" question. A common assumption many therapists have is that we must understand the "why" of clients' actions to help them change their behavior. We learn this early in our training. In coaching, this could not be further from the truth. One very successful life coach, Sherry Lowry, advises new coaches (from a helping professional background) to stop themselves in the coaching conversation if they hear themselves moving into the why. She even goes so far as to recommend they excuse themselves for a few seconds to clear their head so they get back into the coaching perspective and out of the therapy mindset.

Change your therapeutic habits into coaching habits. Much of our actions in therapy is learned behavior and habits. These can be changed with intention and practice. Look at the list of assumptions that you thought might get in your way as a coach. Identify two of them and start working on them today. As we discussed in the last chapter, use a system to monitor your progress and, if possible, work with a colleague to help reinforce each other's change.

Some therapists transitioning into life coaching use 3 x 5 cards attached to their computers or telephones to remind them of the distinctions between life coaching assumptions or behaviors and their traditional therapeutic way of operating. For example, one coach we know has a bright florescent 3 x 5 card taped to her computer that says: "Get out of the past and into the future." Another has "The client is brilliant, not you." A third has "Listen for the WANTS." It is important that *you* find individual ways to help yourself stay focused in the life coaching model rather than the therapeutic model.

Celebrate your transferable skills. When we learn something new, we tend to forget all the good basic practices we already use for our lessons. We often find that therapists who want to be life coaches "forget" all the great skills they already have. These are the gifts and talents that put you out ahead of the non-therapist trained–coach who is going to need to learn how to listen effectively before they even begin coaching. Recognize and celebrate what you bring to this new learning, such as your intuition, listening skills, and reframing.

Some additional suggestions to help you further develop a coaching perspective are:

1. *Stay with us and we'll help you.* Finish this book. We will coach you through the transition and help you further clarify the differences and similarities of therapy and coaching throughout the book.
2. *Get a therapist-trained mentor coach.* If you are serious about wanting to make a transition into life coaching, a mentor coach can help you mark the path. We recommend you hire a mentor coach who has successfully transitioned from therapy.
3. *Sign up for a coach-training course.* The International Coach Federation keeps on their Web site (www.coachfederation.org) an updated list of coach training programs.

In summary, it is critical that therapists who transition to life coaching understand the distinctions between the two professions. Your previous training and experiences will dictate how far you will need to go in order to obtain the coaching perspective. The following table summarizes some major distinctions between therapy and coaching. David Steele, one of our colleagues and a member of the faculty at the Institute for Life Coach Training, has been working with us to further delineate the similarities and differences. His work has been instrumental in developing the tables we have provided. Some of the characteristics listed in the table are beyond the scope of this book and more applicable to a full coach-training program. However, Table 4.1 will help you to develop your own understanding of ways in which the two professions differ.

Table 4.1 **Therapy vs. Coaching**

THERAPY	COACHING
Focus	
Relieve pain, symptoms	Attain specific goals, desires
Restore functioning, adjustment	Create personal fulfillment
History, past	Vision, future
"Why?"	"How?"
Patient wants to move *away* from pain	Client wants to move *toward* goals that are attractive
Context	
Medical/clinical model	Educational/developmental model
Diagnosable illness	Desirable goals, life transitions, or personal growth
Paradigm of pathology	Paradigm of possibility

Table 4.1 continued

Relationship

Therapist as expert; client as patient	Coach as cocreator; a partnership of equals

Orientation

Orientation is process; feelings and inner world	Orientation is outcome, action; inner to outer worlds

Responsibility

Therapist is responsible for process direction, outcomes	Coach is responsible for process; client for results

Style

Limited (if any) personal disclosure	Personal disclosure OK as an aid to learning
Forwards the work through healing, re-parenting, emotions, catharsis	Forwards the work through action, talents, strengths, behaviors, insight into action

CHAPTER FIVE

Reclaiming Your Soul: The Joyfulness of Life Coaching

The most visible joy can only reveal itself to use when we've transformed it within.

—Ranier Maria Rilke

Many therapists and counselors, especially those in private practice, have seen a monumental shift in the profession in the last 20 years or so. Counseling and psychotherapy were, in our opinion, never meant to be part of the medical model, but were seen by many as an art in relating and helping people overcome psychological obstacles in their lives. But, somewhere along the line, the therapy profession was included in third-party payment of services by insurance companies. This allowed *patients* to be covered by the health insurance for psychotherapy if a medical (psychiatric) diagnosis was given to the *patient*. Most therapists did not even use the term patient but instead opted for client, lending more credence to the professional view of therapy as being a nonmedical service. The more we as a profession co-opted to be part of the medical/psychiatric community, the more we got entangled in the managed care system that began infiltrating the profession in the 1980s and then became really intrusive in the 1990s. Almost every practitioner has seen his or her income drastically reduced and paperwork time increased. (The exception here is the practitioner that was "managed care–free" and had a large-enough client pool to survive and even thrive with fee-for-service clients at a reasonable professional fee.)

This shift to managed care has caused great chaos, consternation, and burnout amongst private practitioners to the point where an approximate 10 percent leave the profession each year and another 10 percent wish they could! In fact, *Psychotherapy Finances,* in their annual survey of practitioners, state that 23 percent are taking steps to leave their practice (Klein, 2000). Nineteen percent now list coaching as a service they offer. So, coaching was a professional service waiting to happen and managed care helped it along!

When training therapists about how to add coaching to their repertoire, we have both observed and experienced the powerful impact this career transition (whether part-time or full-time) has had. Once clinicians hear about the possibility of working with high-functioning, highly motivated clients who will pay to have a coach, they get really excited and get a joyful expression on their faces. After all, most of us did not want to work with severely depressed or conflicted persons 100 percent of the time. Didn't you often hope that someone would call you because he or she just wanted to improve his or her life? This allows you to choose more carefully the clients you see for therapy and attract new clients who are candidates for coaching.

As we describe the coaching relationship and the joyfulness of being someone's personal coach, let us first acknowledge that joyfulness can also be part of the therapeutic relationship. Both of us have provided counseling or psychotherapy for years, and we know that there is great joy and gratitude to gained from assisting someone to overcome severe trauma or emotional struggles. We became therapists to really have a positive impact on people's lives and relationships. However, three undeniable factors seem to be at work in the profession of psychotherapy that can lead to a less than joyful experience for the therapist.

1. *Length in the profession.* Psychotherapy with emotionally fragile persons can be draining over the long haul. It is a profession in which the therapists give so much of themselves that professional burnout results if they do not self-nurture.
2. *The degree of seriousness of clients' issues.* Therapists, who often treat clients with serious and complicated diagnoses, are more at risk of burnout due to the psychic and emotional energy required to deal with such difficult and often unresolvable situations.
3. *Managed care.* Therapists, who are trapped in the managed care system, have fewer "approved" sessions with their clients and a lesser amount of reimbursement, plus a reduction in income and more hours of paperwork and increased liability as well. This scenario has led to a large percentage of private therapists looking for ways to make a living in cash-only prac-

tices and needing to add other income streams to their business. Life coaching is a natural transition and can be added along with training, speaking, and consulting.

What Is It That Makes the Coaching Relationship So Full of Joyful Energy?

Isn't it logical that helping someone to experience a better life, a more fulfilling and empowered existence, should foster the experience of joy both for the helper and the helpee? This is a unique quality of the coaching relationship; the energy exchange seems to be less draining on a coach than it often is on a therapist. In fact, we say if the coaching relationship is draining to you as the coach, you are either working too hard on the client's behalf, or the client is not really coachable and may need therapy. We will speak about this phenomenon more explicitly in the next chapter.

Many of our colleagues and graduates of our training program who have shifted from therapist to coach report several factors that have led to a more joyful work experience.

The Work Schedule

Coaches can include a mix of face-to-face coaching and phone coaching and those who do phone coaching can work from home or wherever they happen to be. There are no parking concerns and no need to dress up. Coaches with international clients can even adjust their work hours to accommodate time zone differences and thereby increase their market base to global potential. One former therapist, Barbara Blocker, says,

> I no longer try to fit into somebody else's system or rules about how something needs to be done. I feel good about that because I can control what I do and it fits who I am. I can control my schedule so that it fits my personal life and the balance between work, play, and family is wonderful.

This statement reflects what we have heard from other coaches. You can still be part of your local community and meet people face to face, but your playing field expands to the whole world when you work by phone and e-mail. You still feel very connected with your clients and they with you.

The Ability to Live and Work Wherever You Desire

Coaches who work by telephone with occasional in-person sessions can live in desirous places where building a therapy practice would have been difficult (unless one does therapy primarily by phone, which we have serious objections to and leads to more liability concerns as well). We know coaches who live in very remote communities, on boats, even RVs for a period of time. Telecoaching is not geographically constrained. Some coaches have even exchanged homes with another coach for a month and all they had to do was give their clients a different phone number for that period. Our joy of coaching comes in part from the opportunity to live, work, and play anywhere and maintain a professional presence and above-average income as well. The following story from Christopher McCluskey is a great example of this possibility

> Coaching has been my ticket to an almost entirely different way of life! Lest that statement sound too grandiose, understand that I used to live in a densely populated section of Tampa Bay and had a thriving private practice with a staff of therapists and interns. I was at the office Monday through Friday and saw my family in the evenings and on weekends.
>
> I now live on 440 acres in the foothills of the Ozark Mountains on a little dirt road where the nearest town's population is 215. I do my coaching out of a hunter's cabin I converted into an office, and I work entirely by telephone, e-mail, and fax machine. I eat all my meals at home, interacting with my wife and children (who are home-schooled) throughout the day.
>
> Coaching clients all over the world, I have a flexibility and freedom that would never have been possible in my old practice. I do much of my coaching from the deck of my office, watching the children and horses, petting the dogs, and enjoying the fresh air. I have coached "on the road" while taking field trips with the family, and taught a teleclass series while on vacation this summer at a beach house.
>
> Life in the country was a dream for our family but coaching is what made it possible. I could never have had a private practice out here and, even if I commuted to the nearest town of any size, I'd still be gone the entire day and very tied to the office. Add to that the stress and liability of full-time therapy work, and I can

only say that I wish I'd made this transition earlier! I am more fulfilled and joyful than I have ever been in my life.

The Egalitarian Aspect of the Coaching Relationship

Psychotherapy and counseling require or at least assume a hierarchical
aspect to the relationship. Therapy takes on a "doctor-patient" or "expert-
client" context and requires strict boundaries and ethics in the relationship
outside of the office. In the coaching relationship, the concern of transference and countertransference is not part of the equation. Although our professional training as therapists certainly makes us sensitive to that construct,
we are much freer to be ourselves and be more authentic with our clients.
At a time when Pat's wife lost her hearing in one ear due to a sudden and
severe bout with meningitis, he shared that with his clients when he had to
take a week off to be with her in a nearby hospital. (Many therapists might
also share like this but with more caution and perhaps less detail.) When
coaching resumed afterward, many clients asked about Pat's wife and how
he was doing as well. One client (an attorney) shared with Pat how much
he appreciated "seeing the person behind the coach." The relationship actually became richer because of the ability to be real. Another therapist-turned-
coach, Carol Gaffney, says this:

> As a therapist, you met some wonderful people, but once they
> were your client, they could not be your friend and if you met
> them in public it was always a little strained. But, as a coach, I am
> able to meet wonderful people, know them, and have them know
> me. And we can have lunch, and we can have coffee, and we can
> have a relationship that is not a therapeutic relationship. It is a
> professional relationship that is also a caring relationship, and rela-
> tionships are the basis of business success.

Another coach, Judi Craig, says:

> Coaching is an interdevelopmental relationship where you come
> together as two equals. I think that although some therapists were
> comfortable with self-disclosure in therapy sessions, in coaching,
> clients certainly can know much more about your life and about
> your experiences. And this can even be part of good coaching.

The Financial Rewards

Although we realize that money is not the driving factor in all careers, we also believe that as therapists we have been undervalued and underpaid relative to our expertise, training, and effort. So, the fact that life coaching can command a higher hourly fee or monthly retainer than therapy and require no third-party billing is very inviting. To us, money that is appropriate to the value received for the client is very freeing and more in line with other professions (such as accounting, legal services, strategic planning, public relations). Those that give great value and results should command good fees.

We believe that for the last several years professional therapists on average are making less money and working more. If one subscribed to third-party payers and managed care rules, hourly fees have dropped and paperwork has increased. Even those who are in a private practice may have trouble commanding fees higher than $100 per hour. Of course, there are exceptions to this in large metropolitan cities, but basically this is an average fee. While some coaching clients may not have the resources to pay more than that, most coaches command fees from $100 to $300 per hour—sometimes more for corporate or executive coaching. Coaching is generally for people who are already successful and view coaching as something valuable to assist them in achieving more, making big changes, and living the lives they really want.

Now that we have discussed the four points that lead to joyfulness in coaching, here are some personalized comments from some of our colleagues who have recently trained to be coaches.

> Coaching is my love!! Coaching has been about the power of transformation in my life and in the lives of my clients. It is truly a gift to be a part of my client's journey to the awareness of the innermost part of their being—to the inner sanctuary of their soul. It is there, deep in the soul, where they find peace and joy. It is there that they find their own sacredness, where they know the joy of living and the joy of loving self and others. It is there that they find the passion of living their lives! As they learn the power of their thoughts and the power of intention and visioning, their personal and professional lives are transformed as their dreams are manifested. My life has been changed from one of just existing in a day-to-day routine of work and chores to a life filled with gratitude, celebration, and joy.

My 24-year-old son was killed in November 1998 and the grief stripped me of my energy, resourcefulness, and joy. I stopped taking new therapy clients and, as the people I was treating got better or moved, my practice was dwindling. I did not have the attention to details or tolerance for other people's pain necessary to tackle new cases with my usual fervor and enthusiasm. Since I usually gave 200 percent, my clients still got good therapy when it dropped to 100 percent, but I felt drained and compromised. I went to hear Pat present coaching for a day and felt excited for the first time in years. Within a month, I was in class. Coaching helped me to continue my professional career in a more positive, forward-moving, fashion. I have named my business DreamCatchers after the Indian tradition: if you hang a dreamcatcher over your bed, it will only let the good dreams through. I know I can't keep tragic things from happening, but I can keep them from spoiling my dreams. I have renewed my life purpose: To touch souls deeply while honoring mine. Grief stripped me of my purpose, coaching is giving it back. There is no better definition of joy.

Through coaching and coach training, I have learned to live more in the present. I have noticed that as I literally stop thinking or worrying about what is around the next corner when I am canoeing, that I am more aware of the color of the sky, the warm sun and wind against my cheek, the scenery I am passing, the sound of the birds, the water, the branches blown by the wind, or the canoe moving through the water. This has become a metaphor for my life: When I am not so concerned about what is around the next bend, my awareness and joy in the present moment increase tenfold. Also, rediscovering what I am passionate about helps guide me down the path, providing direction.

My greatest happiness in coaching—the one that carries over long after the session ends—is guiding clients to discover their life purpose and the manner in which they will best use the many talents and gifts they have. It's like seeing them choose the ideal destination for the most significant trip of their lives. After they know where they are going, the path becomes infinitely more clear, the obstacles more manageable, and their own journey much more enjoyable!

This process is especially meaningful for me when I work with mid-life clients who have already explored several options but are experiencing a heartfelt longing for a more satisfying life. When they discover what it is that they are intended to do, when they become acutely aware that their lives have a rich and deep purpose, their happiness is almost palpable. And because it is so contagious, I get to share in their feelings of abundance. It is truly a blessing to behold—and I feel honored to be part of the process.

My first client really made me want to continue on with life coaching instead of therapy. In one and one-half hours I saw a woman in her early fifties change from being so depressed with hopelessness in her voice to having so many new ideas of what she could do that she didn't know what to do first. This does not happen in therapy. A couple days later, she realized she had been depressed for two years and our talk changed her whole life around. She had all these ideas stored in her head but no one ever wanted to listen to her or even encourage her to go for her dreams. Like her, I realize that life just keeps getting better and better. God only knows where I am going but I sure enjoy the journey.

TRY IT!

Assume that the therapy clients you see are whole and capable of greatness and transformation. Focus from that mindset despite the degree of their disturbance or level of trauma. Imagine how you might act or work differently with a specific client if you were his coach rather than his therapist. Assist him to uncover his unique brilliance. Even with clinically diagnosable therapy clients, we believe that the paradigm of coaching and the context of the relationship fosters a potentially more rewarding experience for the therapist and probably the client as well.

For those who are not currently in private practice and who work for a school, clinic, Employee Assistance Program, or elsewhere, we recommend you try the above exercise with your colleagues as well as those who are your clients in whatever way. View everyone you can this week as brilliant and capable of greatness and imagine how you act differently if you viewed him or her in that way.

Are you excited then about reclaiming your passion and experiencing more joy in your work and your client relationships? We believe that adding coaching to your business is a great way to live how you want and help others to live how they want. What could be better? And you can even continue to see therapy clients, but on your terms. Therapy might become more fulfilling, and your clients might experience yourself and your energy in a whole new way!

CHAPTER SIX

The Life Coaching Relationship

When someone prizes us just as we are, he or she confirms our existence.
                              —Eugene Kennedy

The life coaching relationship is like a dance. It starts with an introduction and moves to increasing levels of intimacy. At the first meeting, the coach usually "leads" and helps the potential client to learn the basics, to practice a few life coaching steps. Some distance between partners is common as the dance begins; the coach works to establish the ingredients and principles necessary for a successful relationship.

As the dance continues and intimacy increases, the client takes the lead and the dance can take many forms. Sometimes it is a waltz, slow and clearly delineated. At other times, it feels more like a tango with staccato steps and a fast beat. Perhaps it is rock and roll with loud background music and a driving beat that moves both coach and client forward. Whatever the dance, remember that once the relationship is established, the client should always lead the dance. She picks the music, sets the tempo, and initiates the steps. The life coach helps her stay on the dance floor and encourages her exploration of new steps. This dance and relationship can go on for years, sustained by the client's commitment to seek the life of her dreams and the coach's commitment to help her achieve it. Over time this relationship grows and deepens as the two dancers move masterfully into the future.

The Ingredients of a Successful Life Coaching Relationship

Now that you have a sense of the distinctions and similarities between therapy and coaching and some of the joyfulness we find in our practices, we would like to discuss life coaching relationships. As more is written about coaching in general, and life coaching in particular, we are presented with multiple models and structures for the coaching relationship.

Similarly, the language of coaching is growing and expanding as the field emerges. Phrases such as holding the client's agenda; coaching from the inside out; adding value; forward the action; and the client is brilliant, permeate coaches' conversations and can be found in dialogue at most coaching gatherings and in many coach training manuals. (Many of these terms will be defined in our language later in the book.) Just as the language of counseling became commonplace through the usage of counselors, so too is the language of coaching moving through our profession and the general public. There are so many people inventing and using new phrases and ideas are so openly exchanged that it is almost impossible to determine who said what first.

We want you, as a therapist considering life coaching, to have a sense of the foundation pieces of the life coaching relationship. Similar to what we learned in courses on foundations of counseling, or foundations of therapy, there are essential ingredients for an effective coaching relationship to occur. For the purpose of this book, we have presented what we believe are the ingredients that must be present for the *spark* to occur in the life coaching dance. Not all coach training programs encourage this type of relationship and that is fine. Positive outcomes and good things may happen in coaching without these. However, from the way *we* teach and train, we believe that the following are *significant* components of a successful life coaching relationship.

1. The focus is whole life.
2. The environment is a safe place for client growth.
3. The truth is always told.
4. There is a reserved space, just for the client.
5. The possibilities are limitless.
6. The relationship is soulful.

Let's examine each of these in the context of the life coaching relationship.

The Focus Is Whole Life

Ellis (1998) and Whitworth (1998) have both written about coaching from a whole life perspective. The assumption is that clients don't live their lives in boxes of work, health, relationships, etc., even though they might say they do.

Whatever is going on in one aspect of a client's life impacts other areas of their being. Once clients begin to see this interaction, they gain a wider view of their lives and become more thoughtful about the decisions they make.

It is our opinion that coaches do clients a disservice when they help them excel in one aspect of their lives while ignoring the rest. From our teaching and training perspective, focusing on the whole life is critical. This is why we call our work *life coaching* rather than business coaching, relationship coaching, or some other title.

To this end, we recommend our therapist-trained coaches use some type of whole life assessment in their early sessions with a client, usually after establishing rapport and forming trust. The specific type of assessment is not as important as the product it produces.

Whole life assessment permits the coach to see where the client places their level of satisfaction in significant areas of a balanced life including:

Career
Health
Finances
Relationship
Spirituality
Personal growth (including intellectual and emotional)
Leisure
Family
Continuing education

A benefit to clients is in acknowledging they do have a whole life. We often see clients who are stuck on one part of life, such as work, but blind to the other aspects of their life and how they interrelate. When a coach helps them see things from a whole life perspective, clients are often amazed to discover how some pieces have been neglected or pushed aside.

The Environment Is a Safe Place for Client Growth

If it were easy for our clients to accomplish all the life dreams they have, they would not need us. Life coaching clients want a place where they can approach the lives they have created to this point with the optimism to see new opportunities, the faith in their ability to implement effective change, and the courage to move into the future and take steps toward the lives of their dreams.

As trained therapists, we know that clients are most successful when they feel safe with their helper, and this is certainly the case with life coaching. If our clients are going to take huge risks in order to make significant changes in their lives, they need to feel they have a safe place to leave from and return to—a life coaching relationship is that safe place. Two factors that contribute to that are confidentiality and trust.

Confidentiality is nothing new to therapist-trained life coaches. We know that if clients are going to talk freely about their lives and their goals, they need to know when, if ever, their coach might disclose the content of their conversations. Just like a therapy intake, it will be important during your coaching intake to explain to the client any limitations to confidentiality. At the time of this writing, privileged communication is not granted to coaches, and we do not expect that in the near future. Therapists planning to maintain dual practices (both therapy and coaching) should investigate confidentiality issues further with their insurance carriers and state licensing boards.

You also know what a vital role trust plays in any helping relationship. We show clients we are trustworthy by showing up on time for calls and doing what we promise. We also empower clients with trust by holding them responsible for following through on what they say they want. Clients learn that we are on their side and want for them only what they want and trust them to get it. Trusting our clients' wants provides them with a safe, encouraging environment from which to go forth and take on the huge life changes they want to make.

The Truth Is Always Told

Sometimes in life it seems hard to find truthful people, even in our most intimate partnerships. In life coaching relationships, the truth is always told. From the first intake session, the life coach and client agree to be completely honest with one another.

Effective life coaches want to hear the truth from clients because they know that is when real learning occurs. Clients want to share celebrations and mistakes in a nonjudgmental, safe, and trustworthy place. Clients count on life coaches to tell them the truth and help them sort through the craziness of life's concerns. This includes wanting the coach to be real and not hold back, or just accept what the client is saying to be overly gentle or nice. In therapy we are often aware of the fragility of our clients and try to be cautious with our truth telling. In coaching, we are tactful and direct gently. We act as a mirror for the client to see how they are acting and what they are doing. For example a coach might say: "I've noticed that for the last three weeks you've told me you are going to get a replacement for your administrative assistant. Yet every week you come to our call complaining about being overloaded and overwhelmed at work. When are you going to do something about the replacement? Do you want to develop a plan for that today or is it no longer a priority for you?"

Clients are often aware of how they cover their truth from others and they aren't paying their life coach in order to treat them in the same fashion. Gentle, loving confrontation is part of the effective life coach's tool bag. This does not imply that life coaches tell clients what they should or shouldn't do, instead they remind them of what they said they wanted. This is a relationship without judgment.

There Is a Reserved Space, Just for the Client

Life coaching clients really appreciate that the coaching relationship provides a time "just for me." In this crazy world of multitasking where people do two or three things at the same time and feel good about it, slowing down to focus on what you really want out of life seems a rarity. In fact, it is one of the benefits our clients most frequently cite as appreciating about life coaching. Knowing that once a week they will be contacting their coach and receiving full attention on what they want out of life (their hopes, dreams, fears, wants, frustrations, irritations, and sorrows) is seen as a tremendous gift. This time for the client is similar to the space clients create in their lives for therapy.* A difference is that, in *all cases,* the coaching client *wants* this time and has requested it. Coaching relationships are voluntary—not mandated by any outside source, the way some therapeutic relationships may be. This difference allows the client to savor the space that they have created for themselves and enjoy their own growth.

The Possibilities Are Limitless

Clients direct the life coaching agenda and can bring up anything they wish during the life coaching session. There is room for their dreams and wants in all aspects of their life from the immediate present to the far distant future. This space is so huge that at first some clients can't comprehend the powerful possibilities awaiting them. Life coaches are available to assist clients in figuring out multiple pathways to achieve what they really want. Clients'

---

*This is also the reason many people seek the services of a therapist.

wants may include cleaning their closets; doubling their income; resolving a conflict with an employee; improving intimacy with their spouse; creating a positive relationship with their teenager; leaving a legacy and planning for retirement in three years. Rarely do we ever hear of a client honestly wanting something that isn't in his or her best interest. If this were to occur, we'd simply discuss the situation openly with the client. In fact, the opposite will more likely occur. Clients usually create such big dreams and huge wants that the coach can become breathless keeping up with them. There is room for giant wants and bodacious dreams in the life coaching relationship.

The Relationship Is Soulful

We believe great life coaching goes beyond the surface of the relationship, the techniques, the day-to-day to-do lists. We are especially attracted to what Dave Ellis (1998) refers to as soulful life coaching. We believe the life coaching relationship is, at its best, soulful.

Now, we recognize that not all coaching relationships are soulful. In fact, some coaches, particularly those not trained in the helping professions, might even find this type of relationship uncomfortable and unappealing. It is fine with us that some coaches prefer to operate at a more basic level. Perhaps they are most comfortable working with clients on more surface level issues such as management problems, organization concerns, and time management. We believe all of these are significant, and some of our clients work on them in their life coaching relationships with us. However, we want our therapist-trained life coaches to reach for a deeper, more soulful relationship with their clients. Life coaches who were prepared as therapists are uniquely poised to enter into powerful relationships with their clients. When the coach and client enter a deep and meaningful relationship, great things happen— in fact, miracles can occur. People have totally transformed or recreated their lives. Long forgotten dreams have found their way to become realized. Coaching is about possibilities and the coaching relationship is fertile ground where everyday life can be improved and dreams can grow.

Powerful Life Coaching Principles

Beyond the six significant ingredients of a successful life coaching relationship we have just presented, we would like to offer three powerful life coaching principles that guide our work as life coaches.

1. We believe that our clients are whole and brilliant (even when they don't act that way.
2. We believe that clients want what they say they want (even when they don't act like it).
3. We believe that we are partners and cocreators with clients to help them get what they want.

Let's examine each of these individually.

Clients Are Whole and Brilliant
(Even When They Don't Act That Way)

During our training as helping professionals, we are taught that clients bring an identifiable "problem." The perspective is that something is "broken" and we, as therapists, need to help "fix" the problem through our wisdom, experiences, and answers. We hold the keys that help unlock the door and free clients from their discomfort. As therapists we were trained that we have the skills, knowledge, and expertise to help solve the client's issues. Even when we didn't intend to, we often saw the client needing us to help him find his way. Our strategy would typically be to help the client discover and understand what is broken or not working before we moved to help him look at possible resolutions to the problem.

Life coaches see clients as whole, with nothing wrong, broken, missing, or in need of repair. We also believe that only clients have the answers to their concerns. Therefore, we encourage clients to examine what they *really* want and some possible ways they might start moving forward to achieve it. We wouldn't (as in therapy) concern ourselves with what hasn't been working that kept them from getting what they wanted earlier but rather help them move into the future and create multiple pathways to reach their goal.

For example, if a client were discouraged about his weight, we would want to know his life history and explore how long and why he has had this weight problem; any family problems with weight; any medical factors; what he has done up until now to try and lose weight. We would accept that he knows what he wants and ask him what he would like to do that might help him reach the goal of losing weight. We do not concern ourselves with why he hasn't started on this goal earlier (past vs. future) even though he keeps saying he wants it. We support him as he considers what it would look like to reach that goal and examines various ways he could go to achieve what he wants. Depending on the client, we might teach how to manage weight loss with a general fitness program and help the client discover ways to monitor his progress and celebrate his successes. Solution-focused therapists will recognize some overlap in this example between their training and the coaching paradigm.

We know from our own life coaching experiences that even when clients don't think they have the answer, they do. We've also learned that if we stand by our clients with full belief in their brilliance, they will find not only what they are seeking but also feel better about themselves because they discovered the answers themselves. This attitude reinforces their self-esteem, confidence, and solution-finding abilities, while also increasing the likelihood they will follow through on the solution of their own creation.

Certainly some clients have a desire for someone else to find their solutions or fix their challenges. However, after years of life coaching, we are confident that coaches do their clients a disservice by recommending specific solutions or strategies. As the old saying goes: "Give a man a fish, feed him for a day. Teach a man to fish, feed him for a lifetime."

We recommend coaches always help clients create *multiple* strategies or solutions to get what they want and achieve their goals thereby encouraging self-exploration and discovery. Consider the following exchange:

COACH: What would you like to work on today?

CLIENT: I'm so stressed out! I want to do something about my office, it is driving me crazy!!

COACH: What do you want to do?

CLIENT: I want to clean it up, I can't find anything!

COACH: Okay, you want to clean up your office so you can find what you are looking for. Is that it?

CLIENT: Yes, that would help a lot. I'd feel better and get more done.

COACH: Great, you can have that! What can you do to clean your office so you can find what you are looking for?

CLIENT: I could toss this pile of magazines, journals, and junk mail that I haven't gotten around to reading.

COACH: Okay, what else?

CLIENT: I could put these project binders on the bookshelf in my closet and get them up off the floor where I always trip over them.

COACH: That sounds like it will help you out. What else?

CLIENT: Hmm, I need a good place to put my mail when it comes in. Especially my bills so I can be sure to pay them on time.

COACH: Okay, what else can you do besides tossing the piles of magazines, moving the project binders, and creating a regular place for mail and bills? Would that help you reach your goal of being able to find things in your office and thereby reduce some of this stress?

When clients are encouraged and supported to look inside themselves for solutions and strategies, they learn about themselves, their strengths, and their limitations. We agree with Dave Ellis who says, "Life coaching is about people generating their own answers, not looking outside of themselves for solutions" (1998, p. 3).

Through the life coaching process, clients also discover what they want, what motivates them, what scares them, and when they sell themselves short. Many times clients create a solution and think that it is *the one*. How many times have you known someone who thinks they have *the answer* only to realize it does not work when they apply it to the particular situation? Helping clients create multiple pathways to reach their goals helps them reach their goal armed with many different tools and the confidence that they can create more options if they need them.

Clients Want What They Say They Want
(Even When They Don't Act Like It)

Similar to believing that our clients are whole and capable of getting what they want in their lives, we believe them when they tell us what they want—even if the want might initially surprise us.

When we do a whole life survey with our clients, we discover what they want in many areas of their lives. From that point forward, they keep adding to their wants. We keep a list of what they want in our notes and remind them of what they have said. Even if they tell us a want in December and haven't done anything about it in June, we still believe they want it. For example, let's assume in December a client says she wants to develop a financial plan for her retirement the following July. As her coach, we would make note of that and bring it up in the coaching conversations from time to time ("What are you thinking about that financial plan—are you ready to get started?"). If the client says, "No, not now," we assume she still wants it, even if she isn't making any progress toward that want. This is what many coach training programs refer to as holding the client's agenda.

The life coach's job is to keep clients' wants and make sure they don't get lost. In other words, while clients are clarifying what they want, creating multiple pathways to get there, and going through the day-to-day action plans to accomplish their goals, the life coach supports, encourages, and reminds clients of what they said they wanted in all aspects of their lives (their agenda). At some point, a client may decide that a particular item is no longer something he really wants. Until he says so, the life coach continues to hold it as something the client said he wanted. The life coach helps clients define their mission, purpose, and goals and articulate their dreams, wants, and hopes to achieve the outcomes they desire.

You will be amazed at the scope of wants your life coaching clients take on. Just like your list from chapter 3, our coaching clients have diverse wants. Clients tackle even the most difficult goal with anticipation and hopefulness, because they understand the principles of possibility and the powerful supportive nature of the life coaching relationship. Likewise, we know you won't have a problem with clients' not wanting to do the work. They go for their wants when they are ready.

We Are Partners and Cocreators with Clients

Most coach training programs agree that the power in the life coaching relationship isn't in the coach or even solely in the client but rather in the relationship itself (Ellis, 1998; Leonard, 1998; Whitworth, 1998). Contrasted with therapy where the therapist is seen as the expert, the client sets the tempo in the coaching relationship, and the coach collaborates with the client on goals. To do this, the coach must get out of the way and relinquish the control to the client—a difficult task for some former therapists. The coach's role is to create an environment in which clients can fully focus on their wants, dreams, and desires and the multitude of ways they can achieve them.

Because the relationship is mutually designed, and both the coach and client are intimately involved in making it work, it has the power to nourish both the client and the coach. In fact, most life coaches report an exhilaration and energy associated with their clients. The work of life coaching is sometimes challenging, yet it is common for us to leave a coaching session feeling happier, more fulfilled, and excited than when we began. This is a pleasant change from traditional therapy sessions that could leave us exhausted and questioning if anything positive was happening to forward the client's best interests.

Remember that the life coaching relationship is a dance. You will have wonderful partners (your clients) and a huge array of dance steps (their wants) to explore.

Part III
Powerful Transition Tools

CHAPTER SEVEN

Getting Started as a Life Coach

Our beliefs about what we are and what we can be precisely determine what we will be.

—Anthony Robbins

We've learned that the strength of the life coaching relationship is mutually designed by both the coach and client for the sole benefit of the client's learning and achievement of his or her goals.

The life coaching dance requires you, the coach, to use your intuition, logic, great listening skills, sense of humor, and all of your caring support. It is important to remember that this is a partnered dance, not a solo performance. You must always be attentive to your client's intentions and actions for the dance to be fluid and graceful. As your clients' goals are achieved and their learning enhanced, changes may also occur in your clients' life purposes and values. Your task is to remain flexible and "dance in the moment" with the client. This both supports the client and provides a climate for greater learning.

Just as there are certain basic components present in dancing (music, a dance floor, shoes, special clothing), there are also basic components of the life coaching relationship or dance. Let's look at some of the basics you'll need to set the context of your first formal coaching conversation.

The Intake Session

You are familiar with the initial, scheduled appointment with a client, typically called an intake. In life coaching, intakes may include several forms and vary in location and length, depending on the needs of the client and the coach. Intakes could take place in person or by telephone, and they are usually one to two hours long. You will need to be organized for intake appointments, have several documents prepared in advance, and know thoroughly the procedures you wish to cover in the session. Your intake session is another opportunity to enroll the client in the power of life coaching and help them see what might be. We highly recommend working with a mentor coach before your first intake session. This provides an opportunity to ask your questions and practice some of the language you'd like to use.

First, let's look at some of the standard documents a life coach will use in association with the intake interview:

The Welcome Packet

Often life coaches design a welcome packet for new clients. This includes any forms you will use in the intake plus anything else you would like to give to your client. Some coaches send the client a copy of the welcome packet to complete and return prior to the first session. In this case, the content of the first session would consist largely of reviewing the information provided by the client. We have included a sample welcome packet in the back of the book.

The Life Coaching Agreement

We strongly recommend you create a life coaching agreement *before* you start coaching. This form describes what you can expect from clients and what they can expect from you. Having this agreement is particularly important for therapists who are transitioning into life coaches, regardless of whether or not you choose to continue to practice therapy along with your life coaching business. Developing your life coaching agreement helps you, as the coach, clarify your role in the relationship as well as your expectations for the client. It provides a valuable tool for introducing life coaching specifics to the client. In most cases, we send or give the client a copy of the form before the intake to review. Then, during the session we can clarify all of the various aspects of our agreement and expectations for one another.

There are many variations of life coaching agreements. Most coaches would be happy to show you their forms. The following is a life coaching agreement similar to what we use in our businesses, but it is simply a sample for your reference. We cannot vouch for its legality in your particular situation and recommend you develop your own agreement and have it reviewed by an attorney. Additionally, we recommend you retain the original in your client's file and give a copy to the client. This is a good practice for all your written agreements with clients

SAMPLE LIFE COACHING AGREEMENT
(Your Name Here)
(Your Business Name)
(Address)

Prior to entering into a life coaching relationship, please read the following agreement carefully and indicate your understanding by signing below. If you have questions, consult your coach before signing.

1. I understand that life coaching is a relationship with a life coach that is designed to facilitate the establishment of long-range goals and short-term objectives and the achievement of those goals.
2. I understand that the role of the life coach is to assist me to improve the quality of my life.
3. I understand that life coaching is comprehensive in that it deals with almost all areas of my life including work, finances, health, education, relationships, and spiritual issues. I acknowledge that deciding on how to handle these issues and implementing my decisions remains my exclusive responsibility.
4. I understand that life coaching is for people who are already basically successful, well adjusted, and emotionally healthy.
5. I understand that the confidentiality in the life coaching relationship is limited. Confidentiality will not apply to certain crimes that have either been committed or are planning to be committed. Such crimes may need to be reported to legal authorities. It is also possible that certain topics discussed could be reviewed with other lifecoaching professionals for training and development purposes.
6. I understand that life coaching does not treat mental disorders as defined specifically in the *DSM-IV*. If I have anything in my past indicating that I have an unresolved and serious emotional or physical problem or a mental disorder, then I certify that I am not using life coaching as a substitute for assistance from a mental health professional or a medical doctor.

7. I will not use life coaching as a substitute for counseling, psychother- apy, psychoanalysis, mental health care, or substance abuse treatment.
8. If I am currently in therapy or under the care of a mental health pro- fessional, I will have consulted with that person regarding the advis- ability of my working with a life coach. Additionally, I will inform my coach of this relationship.
9. I will not use life coaching in lieu of professional medical advice, legal counsel, accounting assistance, business consultation, or spiritual guid- ance and for each of these areas I understand I should consult the appropriate professionals. I acknowledge that I will not use life coach- ing as a substitute for such professional guidance. I further acknowledge that all decisions on dealing with these issues lie exclusively with me.
10. I agree to complete regular evaluations of the life coaching process and notify my coach immediately of any concerns.

Signature_____

Please print name _____

Date_____

Address_____

City _____ State _____ Zip_____

Coach's Initials: _____

Copy Given to Client on: _____

Intake Components

Along with the commonly used documents, there are some standard proce- dures or things you'll want to accomplish during your intake session. Depending on the time you allow for intake, you may not accomplish all of these. If not, we urge you to address them in the first couple of sessions. Although not an exhaustive list, we've included a sample of common intake components coaches wish to accomplish. We've also added some samples of language a life coach might use during these parts of the intake session.

1. Collecting all relative client directory information. (You can include a request for this in your welcome packet or develop a form to use as you interview the client.) You will need the client's name, address (home, office), phone and fax numbers (home, office, cell), e-mail addresses, Web site infor- mation, name and contact information of administrative or personal assistant (if applicable), birthday, and names and contact information of immediate family members.

2. Learning what the client wants from you as a coach (today and in the future). Ask clients how they want you to be as their coach, how they envision you helping them. Clarify if they want you to "hold them accountable," "challenge them," etc. Coach: "I'd like you to think about our relationship and how you might like to be coached. I want to give you what you want. We have some options we can consider, let me explain . . ."

3. Learning who the client is. Find out about his or her personal values and his or her life vision or purpose. Coach: "What would you say are some of your values? What really matters to you?" "What is your purpose in life? When you think ahead, do you have a vision of how you'd like your life to be (now and in the future)?"

4. Reviewing what the life coaching relationship is and how it is similar or different from other relationships they may know. During this section of the interview, the coach would help the client understand what to expect in this unique relationship. It is always helpful to ask the client first what he or she knows about life coaching so you have an opportunity to understand his or her perspective and explain how you as a life coach like to work with a client. You distinguish among friendships, consulting, and therapy so the client is clear on how life coaching differs from those relationships.

During this time we also discuss what the client can expect over the course of the coaching relationship (i.e., ups, downs, plateaus, periods where everything moves very rapidly, and periods where he or she may feel "stuck" or in a slump). It is important to normalize this for clients and to reassure them that you will be at their side through all these wonderful highs and possible lows.

5. Teaching how a coaching client can best facilitate growth. This is done through setting an agenda, telling the truth, completing homework, and requesting.

We believe life coaches relationships are most successful when coaches state clearly what they expect from the client. Letting clients know that they are in charge of setting the agenda for each session; telling the truth about what is going on with them and the coaching relationship (from their perspective) and completing all homework they take on are important discussions to have early in the intake. Because there is a lot of content in the intake, we also recommend you continue to follow up with your clients on these expectations through the next few sessions.

Requesting in the coaching relationship is an important tool, and teaching clients about the requesting process is a valuable lesson. It is a great way to help clients get what they say they want without leaving them feeling trapped or required to do something that isn't a fit for them. Coaches often make requests of clients and clients need to understand they have at least three responses they can give back.

For example, a coach might say, "Since you've said this is what you want, I request that you commit to a cardiovascular workout for at least 45 minutes next Monday, Wednesday, and Friday." The client has three options to this request. The client can agree with the request, "Yes, I will." The client can decline the request, "No, I won't." Or the client can propose a counteroffer, "Monday, Wednesday, Friday won't work for me but I'll agree to Monday, Wednesday, and Saturday."

6. *Discovering what is going on in the client's life right now.* Trained therapists are great at collecting this narrative. Clients usually love telling their stories. Clients will tell you their challenges, why they haven't created the life of their dreams, and who they blame along with why they are proud of certain acts, relationships, or accomplishments in their lives. Take good notes as this information provides a great springboard to begin moving the client into the future.

7. *Asking for goals, results, and personal development changes the client would like to work on in life coaching.* You will continue to collect this information throughout the coaching process. Your task as the coach is to begin helping the client focus on his or her wants, in all areas of his or her life so both of you can look out into the future and get a sense of where the client wants to go (today, tomorrow, next month, next year, next decade).

8. *Reviewing your life coaching agreement form and any special policies you have regarding your coaching practice.* We discussed this earlier in the chapter.

9. *Reviewing fee policy.* Collect payment for the intake and the first month of coaching if you use that model.

10. *Requesting a favorite photo.* During our intake sessions we frequently ask clients to pick a favorite photo of themselves and give us a copy. We also discuss why this is a favorite and meaningful photo to them. Later in the coaching relationship it is common for clients to send pictures of new babies, grandchildren, a new home, or even a clean desk or closet to share their lives with us or report their progress in attaining their goals.

Office Management and Fee Collection

Home versus Outside Office

If you already have your own private therapy or counseling practice, you are familiar with office management and fee collection. You'll need to make decisions regarding whether to continue your therapy practice and add a coaching niche or to move completely into life coaching. There are varying opinions regarding the wisdom of maintaining two practices and we suggest you visit with therapists who have made the transition to facilitate your decision. Beyond deciding if and how you will continue your therapy practice, many of the processes you have in place such as filing systems, technology support, and billing procedures will be transferable. We strongly recommend that, even if you do maintain a therapy practice while life coaching, you develop separate documents for your life coaching practice and even consider a separate phone line. Be very clear with clients about your life coaching role and your therapist role in order to avoid confusion and help limit potential liability concerns.

If you are not currently self-employed as a helping professional with an independent office, you have options to consider too. Whether to get an outside office or work at home is a central question for many new life coaches. For this decision, you will want to consider not only your finances and at-home resources, but also the type of practice you wish to have. For example, if you plan on meeting clients in person, having an outside office may make more sense. However, if you plan to do the bulk of your counseling on the phone, you can have a home office, live anywhere, and work in your pajamas if you want to. Both of us work at home and have been successful in defining our space and work schedule so having a home office is a *fit* for us. We both maintain our practices when we travel unless we've negotiated and scheduled a "time out" with our clients in advance. Deb spends six months, spring through fall, in the mountains of Idaho and winters at her place in Maui. A home officeñbased life coaching practice and the addition of a laptop computer make this mobile coaching lifestyle very possible.

If you have never worked from a home office, it is important to consider potential distractions such as children, pets, and noises during your calls and home chores that call you away from your office. Another challenge is the tendency to become isolated. Some individuals feel they need the discipline and structure that an outside office provides. We've known former therapists who go into partnership with another life coach and share an office space by coaching on alternate days. Similarly, a group of independent coaches could rent office space together. A coaching practice does not require a lot of space. A desk, chair(s), phone, computer system, and a fax machine are the basic office needs for most life coaches.

There are numerous resources available with sound advice on establishing a home-based business so we won't go any further into the details. We've included some in the Resources. Before you make a unilateral decision for a home- or office-based practice, we encourage you to explore this topic by both consulting the literature and talking with folks who practice using both models.

Telephone Systems

A telephone headset is the most essential piece of office equipment for any life coach who works on the phone. Clarity of sound and comfort are critical qualities of an effective headset. You must be able to hear your clients and they you without distortion. Depending on the size of practice you desire, you may spend five or more hours on the phone during a given day. Your headset must be comfortable. Cordless headsets provide the flexibility to move about, thus reducing the fatigue of being tied to your desk. Most office supply stores carry entry-level headsets and there are many on-line sources too. Talk to your coach about particular aspects he or she believes are important.

Your telephone coaching practice may function on one telephone line for a while but once you have five to ten clients, you'll want to consider a second line (one for your business and one exclusively for client calls). As your practice grows, you may need a dedicated line for a fax or modem. Voice mail or an answering machine on your business line is also useful. There are increasingly sophisticated office tools programs available for your computer that may provide solutions to your technology questions.

Fee Schedule Collection Methods

We have seen a full spectrum of coaching fees and fee collection methods during our years as life coaches. When you establish your coaching business (which we'll detail in a later chapter) you'll need to ask yourself some important questions that will relate to your fee schedule and collection methods. Here's a little exercise to get you started thinking.

TRY IT!

Ask yourself some of these questions now as you begin to think about your fee schedule and collection methods. Please record your responses in your journal.

1. How many times a month do I want to meet with each of my clients?
2. What is an ideal session length for me?
3. What holidays do I want to have free from work?
4. How will I accommodate client vacations, leaves of absence, or sabbaticals?
5. On what days or hours do I want to coach on a regular basis?
6. How much time, beyond my direct coaching time, do I want to spend on other business-related tasks including preparation and review of sessions and responding to the phone or e-mail?
7. What specific income goals do I want to meet with my life coaching practice?

After reviewing your answers to these questions, draft a tentative "ideal" life coaching schedule and a fee collection policy for yourself. Here's an example of one life coach's "ideal" schedule:

This particular life coach wanted only a part-time practice with the rest of her schedule open for writing and family activities. She elected to coach three weeks out of the month with the first week of the month free from coaching. Additionally, because she wanted structure in her schedule, she chose to coach only on Tuesdays and Thursdays. Clients who couldn't fit into that schedule were referred to other coaches. With regard to hours spent per month with clients, she felt that four hours was her minimum. Therefore, she elected to schedule one-and-one-half hour appointments with clients. She routinely scheduled a lunch and afternoon break into her Tuesdays and Thursdays. This allowed her to have the ideal schedule and lifestyle she wanted while still achieving a successful income stream.

An effective option for new life coaches is to elect to take a few clients for free or a greatly reduced fee while they are getting started. However, be certain to set a clear "introductory period" of free or reduced-fee service so that your client does not expect that this arrangement will continue indefinitely.

As far as collection methods go, you can collect at the time of appointment if you are coaching in person, but for most coaching relationships we recommend you collect in advance for the upcoming month of coaching. This way clients will have already paid and are invested in doing the work, even during a brief slump. Similarly, they are not voting on their coaching with their payment. In either case, you need to be very clear about your policies regarding "no shows" or client-cancelled appointments. It has been our experience that the more time you spend in advance thinking about how you would handle a variety of scenarios, the more likely you are to feel successful about your fee collection policies.

If you do have a problem with fee collection, we encourage you to discuss what is going on with your client immediately and ask when you can expect payment. Your relationship is professional and it is important that payment problems do not get in the way of your coaching. Significant problems are avoided if expectations are addressed in advance and clearly described in the client's materials. The best solution for most dilemmas such as nonpayment is *simply to talk about it*. If the problem continues after discussion with the client, seek some mentor coaching and consider your options. We rarely see this problem occur and it seldom continues after such a discussion.

Your Life Coaching Sessions

How you prepare for coaching sessions is a matter of individual choice, and, over time, we believe you will be a more effective life coach if you routinely schedule time into your calendar and prepare, in advance, for *each* of your coaching sessions.

Here are some general suggestions for preparation before a coaching call.

1. Use a coaching preparation form.
2. Review your notes.
3. Create an agenda for the call.
4. Consciously hold your client as you prepare.

Use a Coaching Preparation Form

One way to prepare for a coaching conversation is to have your client tell you what has happened since the last session and what he or she wants from this session. The best way we have found to do this is through the use of a coaching preparation (coaching prep) form. We believe the coaching preparation form is a "must-have" coaching tool. A sample of this form follows. We strongly recommend that you orient all your clients to the "prep" form early in your coaching relationship; hold clients accountable for completing and returning the form prior to each coaching session. There are several advantages for the coach and the client to routinely use a prep form.

COACHING PREPARATION FORM

Please complete this form and fax or e-mail it to me at least 24 hours before our session

Today's Date: _____

Name:_____

Fax #:_____

Coach Fax and E-mail:_____

....

1. What wins, celebrations, or accomplishments have occurred since our last conversation?

2. What challenges (complaints, energy drainers) do you currently face in your life?

3. What, if anything, did you not get done that you intended to do?

4. What do you want from our session today?

5. Once the session is complete, please write down what you have learned and what you intend to do as a result of our life coaching session. Then e-mail or fax a copy to me.

The coaching prep form requires clients to focus on the upcoming coaching conversation, answer a series of questions, and then fax or e-mail the responses to the coach *prior* to the start of the session. This activity has several benefits. First, it requires minimal time but is critical to helping clients maintain their coaching time as a life priority and helps them show up to the call better prepared and focused. It is fine if they choose to have a different agenda for the call, but the time spent focusing and clarifying what they want is extremely valuable. Second, it gives the coach information, before the call, about clients' celebrations, what they want to work on, what challenges they are facing, and what they haven't done that they intended to do. This sets the stage for the coaching dance to begin!

The final question on the form is completed after the coaching session. It asks the client to reflect on what he or she learned from the session and what he or she intends to do as a result. Answering this question helps clients incorporate the session wants, goals, and insights into intention and future action. It also helps clients hold themselves accountable during the time between calls for what they said they wanted to accomplish. Typically clients fax or e-mail this response back to you.

We have used coaching preparation forms for several years in our practices and are firmly convinced that they significantly enhance the quality of the life coaching session, help clients stay focused on their goals, and continue to move them forward toward their future. They also help us, as life coaches, be better prepared for each of our client sessions. Different coaches develop different forms and have varying expectations about how far in advance of the session they'd like to receive them. You can ask coaches to share their forms with you when you begin to develop your own.

Once clients understand the benefits of using a coaching prep form, they are very responsible about completing it in advance of the session and report that it helps them to be better prepared. With both fax and e-mail options, many clients can submit their prep forms even when they are traveling. An occasional miss typically is not significant.

A few coaches have told us about clients who repeatedly ignore their conversations about and requests for the coaching prep form. In those instances, we advised the coach to consider if this issue is personally significant enough for them that it might warrant a referral of the client to another coach. More times than not, the client who is resistant to trying a new process, such as the coaching prep form, is also resistant to change in other areas. Referral is an individual decision for a coach. For some of us, the coaching prep form is an important tool for providing the client with the level of services we want to offer. For others, it may not be as important. Above all, open conversations should be held with the client from the beginning about anything of this nature that concerns the coach.

Review Your Notes

We take notes during our sessions and recommend you consider doing so too. Effective notes help you account for the many wants that clients tell you they hope to achieve. They further allow you to recall the detail of clients' lives and their changing life goals and values as the coaching relationship advances. We recommend you take down the clients' *exact words* so you can share those with them. Additionally, we routinely offer to take notes for clients and then send photocopies of our notes or summarize key points in an e-mail follow-up to the conversation. This is particularly valuable to clients when they have produced a long list of brainstorming activities or detailed strategies for how they want to achieve a particular goal.

Some coaches keep less extensive notes than we do, but try to include what homework the client has agreed to do, major events coming up for the client, and any goals or daily habits the coach is helping the client track. On occasion, such as in the case of training purposes or a hand injury, a coach might want to consider tape recording a session. If you do consider this option, we strongly recommend you discuss it with the client in advance and specify (in writing) the purpose of the recording and who will have access to its content. Secure the client's written approval to record the session prior to taping. Additionally, prior to any tape recording of sessions (in person or on the phone), you should consult state laws regarding this type of activity.

No matter the format you use, we encourage you to schedule time to review your records before each session and occasionally schedule a time to review the entire client file to assure you haven't lost your focus on the client's wants and dreams. Preparation is a key ingredient in a successful coaching relationship for both the life coach and the client.

Create an Agenda for the Call

We suggest you use the coaching preparation form to create an agenda for the session. While the client is the leader and author of what occurs in a session, the coach is responsible for bringing forth the possibility of the time together. Preparing your own outline or agenda for the session is valuable on occasions where clients just don't know where they want to begin or are not focusing due to external issues. In that situation we might say, "Sounds like you are stuck. I've reviewed your coaching preparation form for today and have some suggestions for where we might begin—would you like to hear those?"

If the client seems hesitant, or at any time shares a different agenda, simply drop your agenda and follow the client's lead. This is sometimes referred to as "dancing in the moment" by different coaches. A sample agenda might look like this:

Call with Teri 6/20/01
Greetings and sharing
Debrief her board meeting last Tuesday (see notes on her prep form)
Ask about celebrations, successes, wins
Consider teaching about agreement keeping
Review homework—exercise one-half hour three times this week? What next?
Ask her about her graduate school wants (notes from January 31st)—does she still want this and what could she do to begin?
Confirm next call date

Consciously Hold Your Client As You Prepare

Prior to a session, take out the photo of your client and have it near you as you prepare your agenda. This is especially valuable for telephone relationships where you may never meet this client face to face. This takes some adjusting for helping professionals accustomed to working in person. Focusing on clients' pictures helps direct your attention and creative energies toward them and creates a bond. We believe we are more effective as coaches when we hold our clients near in thought and spirit as we prepare for our sessions. This is a powerful renewal of our commitment to clients' fulfillment and success.

Other Basic Life Coaching Logistics

Beyond preparation before and after the session, here are a few other logistical recommendations.

Request that Clients Call You

Most coaches prefer to have clients call them (if they practice telecoaching). This encourages clients to take responsibility for their coaching. Occasionally, when an agency or foundation pays us to coach their clients, we call the client and then bill the agency for the call along with other negotiated expenses. Some coaches have an 800-number phone line and ask clients to call them on that number. This is fine, if you choose to work this way, but it is important to remember that you are still paying for the call and must calculate this into business expenses. It is important to have the discussion about who calls whom and who pays for what during the intake session so there is no confusion. We go over this when we discuss fees, but you can also put it in writing in your welcome packet.

Start On Time and End On Time

Time management in a life coaching practice is every bit as critical as in a therapeutic practice. From the onset, be clear with clients that you will start sessions on time and conclude them on time. If a client is late for a scheduled appointment, call her immediately. Usually it is a simple oversight and you can request that she call you right back. We wouldn't bill a client for this brief call unless it was a habit. However, if clients are habitually late, we recommend you discuss this with them as soon as it becomes apparent. Clients who show up late for coaching are often experiencing consequences of being late in other aspects of their lives or are just not being responsible.

Scheduling sessions back to back with preparation time in between for the next one is a strategy some coaches use to manage their time. They know in advance if they let a session run too long they will not be prepared for their next client. Dedicated and effective coaches will not let this happen.

Beyond the Session

We often encourage clients to leave messages on our voice mail or send us an e-mail if they need extra accountability or structure to pursue their goals. Clients sometimes call spontaneously with celebrations. If clients make requests between sessions by phone or e-mail, we try to accommodate their requests in our schedules (such as providing a clarification, sending an article we mentioned, replying to a celebration). However, if a client developed a habitual pattern of always requesting extensive time between sessions, we would discuss this concern and attempt to reach a mutually satisfying outcome. Again, the best solution for most potential coaching relationship problems is early and frequent open dialogue and communication.

Liability Concerns

We are not attorneys and do not profess to have any expertise in this area. As with most helping professions, it is wise to be aware of the potential liability associated with life coaching. Prevention of risk is the preferred approach to liability concerns, just as it is in therapy. We discuss liability in depth during our coach training program but here are several commonsense approaches to possible liability concerns.

1. Practice full disclosure in the intake session and throughout the relationship repeatedly.
2. Execute a written life coaching agreement with the client and review it from time to time.
3. Attend immediately to any concerns either you or the client have.
4. Establish regular, written evaluation of the coaching relationship by the client and the coach.
5. Follow the ethical guidelines provided by the International Coach Federation (see the Resources). If you consider a dual practice as therapist and life coach, we recommend getting a mentor coach who has a similar business set-up.
6. Continue your professional development in life coaching by enrolling in a coach training program.
7. Attend professional conferences and become involved with a peer group of life coaches.
8. Inquire, read, and ask questions about ethics and liability issues, particularly those related to national and state helping professional guidelines. Refer to state and national licensing boards, associations, and professional journals.
9. Regularly check in with clients regarding the relationship and their expectations.
10. Keep thorough notes.
11. Get a life coach yourself!
12. Consult a lawyer when necessary.

Now you have a picture of some key components that comprise the intake interview and regular life coaching sessions. Next, we will examine specific tools that will support your transition into the exciting field of life coaching.

CHAPTER EIGHT

The Basic Life Coaching Model: Skills and Strategies

Most conversations are just alternating monologues. The question is, is there any real listening going on?
—Leo Buscaglia

Both coaching and therapy are more than "just listening" to clients. Masterful coaches, just like masterful therapists, learn various skills, strategies, and techniques that become integrated over time and ingrained in their unique way of working with a client. In this chapter, we will examine the basic structure of the coaching relationship from a simple, yet extremely powerful, coaching model. We will then offer some additional skills and strategies that are useful tools for your coaching toolbox. As you read about these skills, you may be struck with how simple they seem at first glance. Learn these basics first with a beginner's mind, and then begin using them with coaching clients. You will find eventually that using these skills becomes second nature for you. They are also effective tools when you are stuck or are looking for a useful strategy to move a client forward.

The Initial Coaching Conversation

Coaching is best understood as a series of conversations, aimed at evoking the best of your clients and helping them realize what they want to change, improve, or add to their personal or professional life. The initial conversation can occur even before you are hired as a coach. Whenever you have someone interested in experiencing coaching or wanting to interview you as a prospective coach, you can follow the model presented here, even if you only have a few minutes to demonstrate the power of coaching. In this way, you are able to shift to "coaching mode" rather than just have a conversation. Coaching actually becomes a way of being present with people. Remember, before you start to coach you should seek the other's permission by saying, "May I coach you?" or "May I offer some coaching to you?" For example, here is a very common and powerful way to have someone experience coaching when you only have a few minutes. You might meet someone at a party or at lunch, and, having already described what you do as a coach, it is very effective to then have them experience a coaching interchange briefly rather than describe it. Ask the person to describe a goal that they want to achieve, a big dream, or something they want to be different in any area of their life. This is not just problem solving; you can reframe the problem as an opportunity and shift the person's thinking about the future and what they really want in any area of their life.

COACH: Well, Bill, you seem interested in what I do as a life coach. Would you like to experience how coaching might work for just a few minutes here?

BILL: Sure. Sounds interesting

COACH: Tell me something you are struggling with in your life in regard to living the life you really want. This might be a long-term goal or vision, a change you want to make in any area of your life, or something you are putting up with that you would like to change or get completed.

BILL: Well, the biggest frustration with me is my inability to be more organized and I get overwhelmed with all the things I have to do in both my work and personal lives.

COACH: Great. That is so common. So let me ask you, where or how do you feel the most disorganized?

BILL: I guess both with my time and with all the clutter in my office.

COACH: Do you see any way in which those might tie together?

BILL: What do you mean?

COACH: In coaching, our clients begin by "de-cluttering" their life, with both physical and psychological clutter. Loose ends and things that are out of place cause you to feel drained of energy. It is like they pull you away from tasks or unfinished business. Does that make sense?

BILL: Yes! I don't even want to stay in my home office because it is so disorganized. I lose things, have piles of projects, and it just feels chaotic.

COACH: Got it! I have a request. This request is just something I would like you to consider. You can say no, amend my request, or agree to it fully. Ok?

BILL: Okay. I'm listening.

COACH: A disorganized physical space is often reflective of a disorganized mind, and that prevents you from really focusing on moving toward what you really want in your business and in your life. So here is my request. I would like you to take a half-day this week to de-clutter your office. And I suspect you will need help. So I would like you to tell me who you think could agree to do that with you. Could you do that?

BILL: My wife tries to help me from time to time, but it is so overwhelming to her because she does not know where things should go or how to organize it to my liking.

COACH: Do you have a colleague or friend who might be helpful?

BILL: I would be too embarrassed to ask them or for them to see my office.

COACH: Okay. Here's the second part of my request. There are professionals in most towns called professional organizers. Look in the yellow pages, or your Chamber of Commerce listing and find one. They usually do an initial free consultation and can give you a quick design for de-cluttering your office and keeping it more organized. They have seen it all so don't be embarrassed. Besides, I hired one too, and it really improved not only how I worked more efficiently, it also helped me reclaim energy that was being drained away from dealing with piles in my office or time wasted looking for stuff. Will you do that?

BILL: I will. Sounds like I need it.

COACH: Great. Now, a big part of coaching is follow-up and follow-through, so even though you have not hired me, would you please call me or e-mail me and let me know when you will meet this organizer? I really want to know the outcome of your meeting, and I want you to have someone who really cares that this gets taken care of.

BILL: You got it. Thanks.

COACH: That is a quick example of how coaching works. Imagine having a partner who you can contact on a regular basis to help you move on to even bigger goals and desires. The support and accountability is key and, as your coach, I stand for you. I really want you to get what you want in life and for all your possibilities and preferences to become realities.

Demonstrating coaching is the best way for potential clients to really get its power and value. Here, then, is our basic four-step coaching formula that is useful and powerful as the default in all coaching conversations. (These skills will be discussed in more detail later in the chapter.)

Step 1: Listen and Clarify

The first question a coach might ask is, "What do you want?" or "What do you want to accomplish?" Whatever you ask initially should be simple and open-ended to evoke a thoughtful response from the client. Listening *soulfully* to their responses sets the stage for deepening the coaching conversations yet to come. Dave Ellis (1998) describes "full listening" as "an invitation for people to discover their passion—a ticket into the client's soul and a magnet that draws out brilliance" and "soulful listening" as "the kind of listening where you're moved to the depth of your being by what another person says" (p. 33).

Here are some questions and guidelines for you to keep in mind as you listen to your clients' initial responses:

What do you hear?
What does the client need to hear herself say? Or think? Or wonder?
Reframe in order to give perspective and clarity to the client.
Ask evocative and powerful questions.

As the client speaks and answers the questions about his desires, hopes, dreams, and aspirations, you as the coach listen for things to clarify, magnify, examine more deeply, and validate for the client. In a live training, Ellis describes the coaching conversation as one where the client gets an unusual opportunity to say what he has never said, think what he has never thought, and be heard as he has never been heard.

Step 2: Say What Is So

Listen and reflect what you are hearing. An important aspect of coaching is "telling the truth," which means not stepping over anything that you hear, suspect, or want to amplify. Use your intuition and personal radar. Even if you are not totally accurate, the client will correct you and fill in the blank spaces. Telling the truth is *not* analyzing or guessing at causal events as in therapy. It is simply letting clients know what you are hearing, at all levels of awareness, in their words and their energy and in their silence. Saying what is so includes both constructive and supportive comments. It might be areas of potential concerns or things to point out to the client that are over-looked strengths or opportunities.

Listen for the gap. The gap is between where the client is and where she wants to be. The majority of coaching is in the gap. Naming it, giving it structure and clarity, and clarifying what is beyond the gap is where coaching will lead.

Focus on strengths. Listen for the client's strengths, passion, and desire for change. Endorse the positive authentically. Do not make it up but reflect what you can actually support and acknowledge. One of the most powerful aspects of coaching is that someone actually notices our strengths that others in our lives (including us) take for granted.

(Note: This is not the place to be confrontational or to point out obstacles in the client's path. The early coaching conversation is to join with your client and to determine if coaching is something that might benefit her and if she is the right client for you.)

Step 3: Listen More

Once you have said what is so and clarified what you have heard, it is time to listen some more. Allow time here for the client to fully reflect and respond to any "truths" you shared and to expand or adapt her speaking, to be curious, and to be a bit introspective about what you heard. By listening fully and responding truthfully and completely, you invite the client to listen to herself as well. This opens the door widely for the client to see and experience the power of the coaching relationship and the coaching conversations that take place.

Step 4. Request Action

Let's face it. The whole idea of being coached is to make some changes with the help of your coach. So, the final step of every coaching conversation is to request some actions from the client. Make a request for a new behavior or way of being. Ask him to make a small step toward the changes he wants to make. For example, he could clean up some of the clutter in his office. Ask him to take three steps toward the larger goal or big dream that he has. Break it down into smaller steps and request that he tells you what he will do and when he will do it. That is the heart of coaching. Stretch the client to do what he has wanted to do but has not had the push to do it. Ask for some new behavior, something creative and *outside the box*. The old way hasn't worked or he wouldn't be seeking coaching.

Remember that best way to ask for action is to make a request, not to offer a suggestion or advice. Frame your request in such a way that clients can agree, disagree, or adapt what you are asking. That way, they own the action steps as theirs.

Listening As a Coach

Listening as a coach is different than listening for pathology, history, pain, and psychological blocks. In life coaching, one listens *to* what the client is saying (and not saying) and listens *for* unspoken wants, desires, passion, and possibilities. Remember, coaching is about designing a life and a future desired by the client, by listening *for* what it is that they want most.

A masterful coach listens for clients' visions, values, commitment, and purpose in their own words and intent. To listen *for* is to listen for the gap, an unrealized passion, or an obstacle. The coach listens with keen attention and with a purpose and focus that arises from the partnership that was designed with the client. The coach is listening for the client's agenda, not what the coach thinks the agenda or direction should be.

Listening for the solution is an obstacle to great coaching! This tendency blocks the powerful process of discovery and uncovery and the creative ideas that come from the coaching conversation. We natural helpers often jump to probable solutions that might work, but the power of coaching is in bringing out the best in our clients, not just giving it to them as a quick fix. In sports, athletic coaches do not just tell athletes what to do but coach them to find the way that works for them, within tried and true methods of practice and training. Coaching is not advising or training. That can be part of the overall relationship, but it must be labeled as such and used at a minimum. In other words, clarify your role if it is more than coaching.

In addition to listening to and listening for clients, great coaching also uses a type of listening that we call listening *with* clients. This is listening consciously and deeply from the heart to what is evoked in us by the client's words, energy, and being. Pay attention to the images, emotions, and sensations that resonate within you. These are the sources of great wisdom and breakthroughs that are available to you and your clients.

Deep listening as a coach involves all three levels of listening described above and is very different from how we listen to a therapy patient or a truly mentally disturbed individual. Deep listening can also be powerful in everyday living with those we really care about.

TRY IT!

Try deep and soulful listening as a coach this week with three different people. Ask them for feedback on how you did.

Use the basic coaching formula with at least one person this week and notice how you did. Get feedback from that person as well. How was it different than therapy? What happened as a result of the action request? How did you feel as the coach?

Telling the Truth As a Coach

The second step in the basic coaching formula is *saying what is so,* or telling the truth. In coaching parlance, this does not mean to confront, question the client's integrity, or make the client wrong. Telling the truth is about pointing out potential incongruencies or intuitions about problem areas *and* pointing out the client's strengths through acknowledging and endorsing. As a coach, say what you mean; just don't say it mean!

In coaching, we focus on strengths and then create actions to create new strengths while building on those already present in the client's life. We make a distinction between complimenting, acknowledging, and endorsing. In fact, you might think of these on a continuum:

Complimenting ⇨⇨⇨⇨⇨ Acknowledging ⇨⇨⇨⇨⇨ Endorsing

The arrows imply that as you move from left to right, there is increased depth and specificity in coaches' comments. Complimenting someone is a good habit to have—about what the client did, what she wore, how she looks, etc. Acknowledging goes a bit further and includes comments about a person's specific behavior or way of being that shows up in something she did. When you acknowledge someone, you speak a little deeper about her being and the *who* more than the *what.* Endorsing goes even further and includes a deeper level of articulating than acknowledging and includes some intuitive comments about the heart of being. An endorsing comment is more about the *who* than the *what* of the person being endorsed. It is targeted more to *being* than *doing* or *having.*

A very powerful coaching skill is being able to acknowledge authentically or endorse qualities, actions, abilities, or gifts that clients exhibit as their

The Basic Life Coaching Model   103

stories unfold. The power is in the delivery of the truthful message about what you hear, see, or intuit as the coach that the client most likely rarely (if ever) hear about their self. Here is an example.

A client named Joan comes to you for coaching and wants to be able to grow her business in a way that is not as challenging and overwhelming as her current job. She feels unfocused, a little lacking in business acumen, and generally unsure if she is on the right track. She feels that her life is out of balance, with her business leaking into her personal and family time. After listening to the client's story and desires for several minutes, you as a coach could say something like this:

Complimenting: Joan, I want to tell you that you are doing the right thing here. You are focusing on what really matters. Way to go! (Complimenting is a positive comment but too ordinary and shallow for powerful coaching.)

Acknowledging: Joan, as I hear you share your dreams as well as your frustrations, I want to acknowledge you for having such a great vision and for being willing to seek help. You have big plans and you are smart not to try it alone. (Acknowledging is about validating what the client is saying and about who they are. It speaks to both *doing* and *being*.)

Endorsing: Joan, I have to tell you how struck I am by how you reveal your vision. Listening to your words and feeling your passion really help me see and sense you as a very caring being that is up to big things. You have eloquence in your style that is unique and expresses the joy and excitement in your life's purpose that you want others to experience in their lives. Thanks for letting me experience that part of you. (Endorsing is very close to acknowledging but goes deeper. A coach endorses by authentically commenting on the uniqueness of the client in reference to the current discussion of their goals. It is mostly about who they are, the human being more than the human doing.)

Action as the Goal of Coaching

As we stated earlier, action is the result that all clients want in coaching and although there are action-oriented approaches to therapy, designing action plans with clients in coaching is a cocreative process that comes from the coaching conversations.

Coaching is a way to assist your clients in charting their journeys. There is a saying, "You cannot change the wind . . . but you can adjust your sails." That is partly what we do as coaches. We help the client make adjustments with planning, focus, and follow-through (action). As coaches, we do not design the course for our clients. They may create and design their futures with our action requests or suggested experiments. We really lead from behind. However, we might be familiar with clients who express resistance to action and move from one issue to the next to avoid making the necessary changes in their lives. If you have a client like that in coaching, you, as the coach, will want to explain that the process of coaching is to assist him in defining his vision and clarifying his goals to make his life as fulfilling as possible. If you have clients who are unable to improve their focus and action in coaching, they may not be coachable (yet) and they might need an appropriate referral to a therapist to help with the resistance—coaching being something they can return to.

Coaches work on both long-term vision as well as short-term actions for the next week, the next day, or even the next hour. People tend to get stuck in the future or the past. The purpose of action requests in coaching are to help them carry out actions in the present so they are more likely to achieve their the desired future. As coaches, we assist our clients with designing a future path, but we also create actions for living in the present. The magic of effective coaching lies in the ongoing relationship, but the outcomes come from built-in accountability to the coach. The key coaching questions toward the end of any coaching call or session are, "What will you do? By when? And how will I know?" This format creates accountability for the client to be purposeful and active before the next coaching conversation.

Action requests in coaching are often balanced between doing and being. Clients want to do something differently in their life or work and they often forget the *who* and focus more on the *what*. Carl Jung said, "Your vision will become clear only when you can look into your own heart. Who looks outside, dreams. Who looks inside, awakens" (p. 57).

CHAPTER NINE

Advanced Coaching Skills

Excellence demands that you be better than yourself.
—Ted Engstrom

Learning lots of skills and techniques in coaching is similar to learning to drive a car. You will very likely be conscious of using them and even somewhat structured at times when trying to use them. However, eventually, you will forget the details and just coach. All the while, these skills will become integrated into your coaching style and are available as references or reminders when you feel you need more structure or strategy. We find it helpful to have lots of coaching tools to help us stay flexible and not get stuck in a few default methods of coaching. Trying new tools keeps our coaching fresh and exciting. We believe that what really guides clients and their progress toward the life of their dreams is the coaching process, not the coach!

Coaching is more than just applying the principles and practices of solution-focused counseling to a coaching client, although many of the techniques and questions can be helpful. Coaching is much more than solving problems or eliminating barriers. While this may be one of the reasons clients seek coaching, life coaching is also much more than solving problems. As we have stated, life coaching is about creating the life one really wants to live. It goes beyond problem solving and into life design and fulfillment. As problems are resolved and barriers reduced or removed, clients move closer to their goals. Being free of these former obstacles allows and encourages coaching clients to be empowered, to be "energized" and on purpose for what they want to be different in their life and are therefore able to discover ways to realize their intentions.

Skills and Tools for Empowering Clients

In chapter 8, we discussed the importance of listening for strengths and acknowledging or endorsing the client. This should be reviewed, as these skills are the basis for empowering clients. First, be clear with clients about the existing strengths or gifts that they already present; second, build on those skills and talents; then, in your coaching, choose from any or all of the following skills for empowering clients:

Being curious
Standing for
Reframing
Never make the client wrong
Preferencing
Possibility thinking
Powerful questioning
Purposeful inquiry
Compassionate edge
Use of metaphors, stories, and analogies

Let's examine each of these.

Being Curious

One of the unique characteristics of a great coach is to be curious with clients. Being curious implies a level of detachment from the outcomes and allows the coach to listen to what clients say they want and what they say gets in their way. This helps clients be in a nonjudgmental space about what they want to undo or decrease, what they want to do more of or increase, and how they want to *be* different as a person. Using curiosity as a coach helps take you out of the expert role and helps you join in the clients' adventure of discovering what it is they really want before the temptation to find solutions or actions happens too quickly. This is empowering because a client's response to your curiosity very often leads to his or her own self-discovery. We have all experienced feeling more charged up when we have discovered our own answers or direction. Curiosity helps the coach stay out of the way and assists the client to uncover or discover his or her own brilliant answers or solutions. It is a powerful stance for the coach to know that clients have the answers but seek the benefits from the coaching process to assist in their discovery.

Example: The coach might say, "Mary, I am curious about your desire here. What is it that compels you to seek this goal? How will your life be better when this is achieved?" Curiosity is a state of coaching that allows the coach to ask powerful or evocative questions from a nonjudgmental and inquisitive context.

Standing For

Many of the coaching skills presented here are ways to empower clients by validating and acknowledging a part of their being or specific behaviors. Standing for emphasizes *what* the client wants in her life rather than who she needs to be to get it. As a coach, you "stand for" a client's dreams and desires simply by remembering them for the client and believing in the possibility of realizing them. Who else in a person's life does that on a consistent basis? You remind clients of what they said they wanted, and you remind them of their deepest desires, even when (or especially when) they get distracted. As the coach, you serve as a container for your client's visions and the goals and objectives needed to achieve the change she really wants. In the coaching relationship, you stand for the client and her wants, even if they are not what you would want or if you are not sure the client can achieve them. Unless clients' desires border on the unethical or illegal, you must suspend judgment and stand for the possibility and passion clients have for their goals. After all, we all know stories of great achievements accomplished when others thought they were unattainable, because someone took a stand for what he or she believed was possible.

Standing for is a skill that shows up more in the way you relate to the client and in the sacred space you create in the coaching conversations, rather than being a technique or tool that you learn how to "use."

Example: A coach might respond to a client's big dreams and aspirations this way, "Pete, I want you to know that I hold your dreams for you in our relationship. We may from time-to-time focus on more short-term or even immediate outcomes, but I stand for your larger goals that are the crucible in which all these smaller accomplishments rest."

Reframing

This is a skill that most modern therapists are familiar with and it is an equally useful skill in coaching. In reframing, you find other words or descriptors for something that appears to be a challenge, problem, or deficiency in the client's view. You place the behavior or perception, as articulated by the client, in a new context or *frame*. This allows the client to see whatever the situation or concern is in a new way. Rather than viewing the problem as a weakness, it can be seen as an opportunity for learning.

Example: The client says, "I get so distracted from my goals much of the time. I sit down to write my workbook for my seminars and schedule more presentations, but I just get stuck and go nowhere."

The coach replies, "It seems to me that you are really the visionary and leader in your trainings. You are not the person to work with the details. What if you find someone to take on the details of the planning, scheduling of the seminars, and finding a cowriter for the workbook? Your strengths are in the *inspiration* and delivery of the material, not in the *perspiration* and the details of the scheduling and planning."

Great teachers and mentors have always used reframing or metaview in their teaching. In the movie *Dead Poets Society,* Robin Williams, a prep school poetry teacher, uses reframing masterfully. He asks his class to come up one by one to the front of the room and stand on his desk in order to give them a *different view* of the classroom. That is a visual description of what reframing does with coaching clients. We, as coaches, ask clients to look at their dilemma with a different frame around it, to look at it from the future that they want, or to view it from a meta-position, as if they are above themselves looking at themselves. Practice using reframing in your practice and notice how often and naturally you begin to use it as a method for helping your clients change their perceptions. Please note that this is not just "sugar coating" a negative situation—it puts the situation in a new framework, which then allows and encourages the client to seek different action choices based on revised perceptions.

Never Make the Client Wrong

This may be the most difficult skill in coaching. We, as humans, are so familiar with finding fault or correcting others' mistakes, especially if we think we know the truth or right answer. As a coach, you are hired to evoke the client's brilliance, which implies that he is brilliant, but may not fully express it in his life. When a client does not follow through on an assignment or stick to his commitments, the coach needs to examine and speak with the client about that behavior. However, the key skill here is to conduct the discussion in such a way that the client still feels supported even while having a conversation or query about something he did not do.

Example: A common occurrence in coaching is for the client to have failed to complete the goals and commitments she agreed to for the time between sessions. As coaches, we might respond in this way: "Cecilia, I hear that you did not complete the tasks that you set out to do this week. What got in the way and how can we discover together some new strategies for your success with this today? Or maybe we need to change the goals. What do you think? I really want you to have success with the changes and accomplishments you seek."

It is very important for the coach to focus on what clients want and not what the coach may think they need. If clients do not have a clear picture of what they want to be different in their lives, then that is where the coaching begins—to discover that. You can remind clients of their objectives and desires and ask how you can best coach them to do what it is they want to do and not make them wrong in the process. After all, whatever happens is just results, not failure, and results can be examined as learning opportunities. As coaches, we can point out what did not happen that the clients said was desired and ask if they want to recommit. We can inquire what got in the way, or explore a new direction that clients may want to go in. All of this can be done in a neutrally charged manner and a very caring way, without making clients feel wrong or a failure. There is probably enough of that in their lives already! Accept clients for who they are, where they are, what they do, and how they show up while helping them to discover ways they can change behaviors, habits, relationships, or actions. *Never to make the client wrong* is another gift we give our clients through a special coaching relationship.

Preferencing

Clients often come to coaching with a long list of things they think they *should* be doing, *ought* to have, or *need* to change. These are usually beliefs they have developed from the influence of other people in their lives, books, talk shows, and experts. Remember, coaching starts with the question "What do *you* want?" and keeps at that question until clients have broken through the list of shoulds, oughts, and needs. Using the skill of preferencing, the coach encourages clients to look at their various desires for change and articulate what they would prefer without initially providing any particular rationale. Preferencing helps clients increase their awareness of how they have been limiting themselves unconsciously.

The use of preferencing in coaching is simply a linguistic shift that allows clients to be less attached to the outcome. For example, the coach might say to a client, "Stephen, I see how upset you get when the meetings with your team do not go as you intended and surprises occur that seem to throw you off-track. I would request that you have a *preference* for the outcome you would like and move toward that, possibly even state it out loud. However, I would also suggest that this would free you up to "go with the flow" of the meeting and not be distracted if your preferred outcome changes or is amended. Could you try that this week?"

A conversation that both of us often have with our coaching clients is about making distinctions. Clients can get too attached to big dreams. The skill of preferencing assists the client to *desire* these dreams but realize that it is only their preference. We cannot predict the future. Although it is very wise to plan and to chart a course toward a destination, things happen which can knock us off course. So, coaching clients toward the distinction of preference over need is crucial.

One of Pat's favorite quotes that has been a compass in his life is from *Notes to Myself* (1970) by Hugh Prather:

> If everything were to turn out just like I would want it to, just like
> I would plan for it to, then I would never experience anything
> new: my life would be an endless repetition of stale successes.

In their wonderful book *Recreating Brief Therapy: Preferences and Possibilities* (2000), John Walter and Jane Peller state that they now work from a position of wonder and curiosity. They are more personal consultants to their clients to help them discern how they would *prefer* to live their lives and to explore the *possibilities*. They even go so far as to suggest to helping professionals that the field "replace *therapy* with *personal consultation* or some other equivalent term" (p. 15). Sounds like coaching to us!

Possibility Thinking

A powerful part of a coach's job is to be a possibility thinker with the client. As coach, you partner with clients in seeking possible solutions or new strategies to help them make the changes they want in their lives. Bill O'Hanlon (1999b), a therapist and writer we both admire, developed an approach to therapy he calls possibility therapy—a humorous and passionate approach to action-oriented therapy. This approach could be a variation on the old technique of brainstorming, but it is different in that the process is coengineered by client and coach. When clients are stuck in a habitual way of thinking or a problem-focused orientation, possibility thinking encourages them to consider alternatives or other ways of looking at the focus of their perceived problem or dilemma. Possibility thinking offers clients a method to suspend their current belief system and to explore a much larger field of potential choices. This may also work concurrently with the use of powerful questions like "What if?" or "What would it be like if?" or leading clients to view their possible futures with different courses of action and expectations. Possibility thinking can also be done in a light-spirited manner that we believe helps take the emotional attachment and seriousness out of clients' current views of their situations. Part of the real joy and excitement that comes from coaching is that the context is about challenging our self-imposed limits. Possibility thinking as a coaching skill is well received, fun to use, and often transformational for the client.

Example: The client might say, "I am so frustrated with my computer. It keeps freezing up and the e-mail server loses outgoing mail. I don't know what to do. I hate technology!"

The coach could respond, "Marcia, I know this is frustrating. Let's brainstorm together some possibilities to remedy this, okay? Why don't you start with two or three things?" (Note: as a coach we then encourage the client to think of a couple of possibilities, then we might suggest a couple of others and try to come up with a list of eight to ten possible solutions which often include some crazy ones like "you could take your computer out back and smash it with a hammer.") The point here is to get the client to think of strategies she has not thought of and to stretch them into new possibilities. As the coach, we would use language like, "This is just my best thinking here in the moment. I don't know if this would work or not, but what if you hired a computer tutor to come to your house each week?"

Powerful Questioning

Most therapists are very familiar with the use of questions to evoke information from clients or perhaps to lead to new patterns of thinking about their difficulties and how they might be transcended or resolved. Solution-focused therapy, Ericksonian hypnotherapy, and neuro-linguistic programming all teach methods using powerful questions. "Suppose one night, while you were asleep, there was a miracle and this problem was solved. How would you know? What would be different?" (de Shazer, 1988). Steve de Shazer and the Milwaukee Brief Therapy Institute have become known for their famous *miracle question,* which is actually an evolution of the big question taught in Adlerian psychology (1998).

Frankly, we believe that much of the work of de Shazer and associates could insert the word "coaching" and all of their theories are applicable to this new paradigm of possibility. However, it is important to keep in mind that although many of the techniques of solution-focused therapy and even Ericksonian or neuro-linguistic programming could be applied in coaching, that does not necessarily mean that coaching is the paradigm. Simply working from a stance of possibility does not make what you are doing coaching. Though de Shazer, O'Hanlon, and others share similar posturing as coaches, other aspects of their practices are distinctly for therapy issues and not coaching. Coaching skills can be used with therapy clients, but coaching is a cocreative relationship and this context is what qualifies it as coaching.

Powerful questions in coaching are meant to stimulate clients' thinking. Powerful questions are usually questions to which the coach does not already have the answer. They are meant to forward the exploration of information and possible behavioral choices available to the client. These questions in coaching are meant to expand the notion of curiosity and wonder so both the client and coach can keep their own agenda in the background as much as possible.

Examples of powerful and evocative questions are: "If you had all the money you needed, what would you be doing?" "If you only had one month to live, what would you do differently?" "What would be different in your life if, one year from today, your life was exactly like you would like it to be?" "How would you know when you have gotten what you want?" When a client is unclear as to what he wants, you might ask, "If you did know, what might your response be?"

A client might say, "I want to increase my sales and yet not have the business overwhelm my family and personal time." And the coach would reply, "What would an ideal week look like for you if you had plenty of work time and your desired family and personal time?" Or, "How would you know when you had a good balance between work and personal life?" A powerful question evokes deeper thought from the client and is usually a question the coach does not know the answer to. It is to explore possibilities and new ways of being or doing for the client.

As you practice, you will not need to rely on this list but will be proficient in creating your own questions spontaneously during conversations with clients.

Purposeful Inquiry

This means asking questions for which you want an answer not now but later after the client has used the question to focus their thinking. For example, we might have a client who is very driven to make a career transition to a new job or an entrepreneurial venture that would be more "satisfying." For this client, we would request that she consider this inquiry for the week between our sessions—"What would the components of a more satisfying life or career be?" We tell the client not to answer that question but to use it as an inquiry and to write down all her thoughts about it during the week. This type of question often leads to some very powerful insights and information that can catapult the client into exciting life changes. Purposeful inquiry might be compared to the Socratic method, where an in-depth examination is enabled by staying focused on questions instead of looking for immediate answers. Socrates said, "A life unexamined is a life not worth living." Most of the time, the inquiries are the same as the powerful questions mentioned in the previous technique, but these inquiries are for delayed and in-depth thinking rather than answered on the spur of the moment. You, as the coach, can create these inquiries in the moment toward the end of the call (or session), or you can have several standard inquiries that you compile and choose from as you see fit. Either way, the inquiries lead to incredible shifts in clients' thinking and contribute to some very stimulating coaching conversations. Purposeful inquiry is a technique of coaching that is both fun and illuminating. Bear in mind what the poet Rainer Maria Rilke (1904) had to say about the value of questions:

> Be patient toward all that is unsolved in your heart. Try to love the questions themselves. Do not now seek the answers which cannot be given. Because you would not be able to live them. And the point is to live everything. Live the questions now. Perhaps you will gradually, without noticing, live along some distant day into the answers. (p. 27)

Purposeful inquiry is often the same kind of question as a powerful question, but is posited to the client to contemplate between sessions. It is not to be answered in the moment, but used as a question to think about, talk about, write about and to come back with the results of the inquiry. For example, the client might say, "I really feel frustrated in my career, like I am stuck in quicksand and not able to move." The coach would then respond,

"I would like to give you a purposeful inquiry this week, okay? What would be different if you got out of the quicksand? Use this inquiry this week and report back to me. At the next session tell me what thoughts or images or feelings you had about this exercise."

Compassionate Edge

There are times when a coach needs to be truthful in a way that could appear confrontational. We like to think that difficult messages can be delivered in the coaching relationship with a compassionate edge or what we call "care-frontation." When would you use the compassionate edge? We have used it to remind clients of our personal or professional boundaries. Although it does not happen very often in coaching, a client might overstep your availability and call for long conversations between scheduled appointments or send you very long marketing plans or business forms that you have not agreed to review in your coaching agreement. If you feel overwhelmed or that your time and coaching services are being overused, you need to bring this up with the client. You might also use this skill when clients engage in unhealthy or repetitive behaviors that block their success. Using the compassionate edge means that you can be truthful, without being mean or nasty. Compassion means you give the information in a sensitive way and edge implies that it might be blunt or "right to the point." You model good coaching for clients with this skill, and you also teach them a useful skill in assertiveness in their own life. If you tell a client up front that there might be a time when you need to be direct but your intention is never to be hurtful or uncaring, it is well received when you deliver it.

For example, you might say, "I have something I need to say and it needs to be direct. I am going to say it with compassion because I do not want it to be misconstrued. However, if it does not come out right, I will clean it up." (The coach will continue the conversation until the intent of the message is clear and understood.) That way the client, who you have already built good rapport and trust with, will already know your intentions. The conversation can then continue in an open manner until the communication is clear and resolved of conflict. This is a skill that takes practice but is crucial to successful coaching. We like to say humorously that this skill is not from the Bobby Knight school of coaching (University of Indiana), but more from the Roy Williams school of coaching (University of Kansas), without undue emotional expressiveness. College basketball fans will understand this analogy. If you don't, don't worry about it. Can you think of a time when you might use a compassionate edge? Can you remember a time when someone else used it (or could have) with you?

Masterful coaches get quicker and more powerful results because of their willingness and comfort in using a compassionate edge. Compassionate edge comes from the coach's unwillingness to tolerate mediocrity and yet continue to be compassionate and empathic with the client. Clients expect coaches to guide them to excellence; using this skill can help because it moves clients to acknowledge unspoken truths, behaviors, or habits and therefore transform them into more purposeful actions.

Mastery of the compassionate edge has benefits for the coach as well. Once you become skilled and comfortable with it, you will find that you will attract high-powered clients who expect this edge from their coach. They are not just learning the skill; they are high achievers, who expect the best from their coach, because they desire the best in their lives.

For example, a client might say, "I sent out ten letters this week and had two conversations with people about my new business." The coach might respond: "Jim, I really want for you to have the success you seek. *You have set the bar too low.* I would request that you commit to sending out one hundred letters this week and having two conversations a day describing your new business. You have to stop being a secret and I want to raise the bar higher for you. Will you accept this challenge?" This is an "edgy" and aggressive approach by the coach, but is used when the challenge can be done compassionately and nudge the client to greater action.

Use of Metaphors, Stories, and Analogies

Here are techniques that many therapists already use in their approach to psychotherapy. Whether these are natural for you or whether you need to learn how to use them better, metaphors, stories, and analogies are very powerful.

METAPHORS
Dictionaries define a metaphor as a figure of speech in which a word or phrase denoting one kind of object or idea is used in place of another to suggest a likeness or analogy between them, as in "drowning in money." At a conscious level, the client has a highly personal and bonded experience of the coach's understanding. At a deeper level, the message can bypass the client's awareness and go directly to his unconscious—the seat of 95 percent of perception and emotion and the generator of behavior.

Metaphor making is going on all the time, effortlessly, in country songs, on playgrounds, in your own household. Start to be aware of the metaphors you use naturally and the ones you hear used around you. Collect and treasure metaphors; listen for new, surprising ones and for whatever vibrates your tuning fork. Here are some examples used in coaching situations.

1. Your client is a distracted businessman who wants to use his time more wisely and have energy for work as well as his personal life. In getting to know him, you learn that he plays blues guitar for his own pleasure. Remind him that if he practices time management skills one step at a time, he will eventually use them automatically, like making a C-chord effortlessly on the frets without thinking and he will experience harmony between work and home.
2. Your client has a passion for woodworking. He tells you how stressed he's been, trying to get a project finished in time for his wife's birthday, and he knows that hurrying makes mistakes. You say, "Charlie, how can you tell when the top of that cabinet is level?" He describes using a carpenter's level. You answer, "So, Charlie, what can you do to ease up and get your own personal bubble to just settle down, right between those lines?"
3. Your client is a Wonder Woman executive who has a hard time slowing down, but desperately wants balance in her life. You suggest that she spend time on the weekend in "canoe mode," just trailing her fingers in the water and letting life take her where it will for the day.

What do these examples have in common? They establish rapport and offer an embedded, implied suggestion. Roz Van Meter (personal communication, October, 2000) says, "I had a hyperactive telecoaching client who kept speaking in such staccato rhythms that I had trouble focusing on his session. I asked him what kind of music his brain was playing. 'Well, some kind of salsa, I guess.' I asked him to take a long, slow breath and change to an easy-listening station. He took a deep breath and calmed down. His voice fell half an octave in pitch and slowed, we reconnected, and he was focused again."

Metaphors, analogies, parables, and allegories can be woven into a tapestry as elegant as a magician's cloak and as powerful as his wand. An experienced coach or therapist can

listen for the client's own metaphors to tell you *who* he or she is;
match his world with parallel metaphors to let him or her know you understand;

use metaphors to confirm his or her desires and goals (*what*);

construct allegories linking *where* he or she is to *where* he or she wants to go; and

create parables and dream weaving to create the map (*how*).

Stories—legends, myths, epic ballads—have been the teaching method of transcended masters from Aesop's fables to Greek tragedies to the Bible to Sufi stories and family stories. Once you truly understand what the client wants and what stands in his or her way, you can become a storyteller too. "You know, I once knew a man who . . ." or "My Aunt Irma used to tell us about . . ." and then you can construct a parable that parallels the client's dilemma and offers a solution—remember, not an exact match, but a parallel one.

Many of us may have learned to hone our skill in using metaphors, stories, and analogies by reading of the magic of Milton Erickson and his followers (Bandler & Grindler, 1975; Haley, 1986; O'Hanlon & Martin, 1992; Zeig, 1994). Powerful applications of Erickson's wizardry are applicable to coaching. He, after all, was more of a life coach than a psychotherapist.

STORIES

Some coaches are skillful storytellers and are able to relate a true story or create one that teaches a point to be explored in coaching. Coaching stories are like those in *Chicken Soup for the Soul* (1993). They are heartwarming, inspirational, and have a moral or point that relates to the client's situation.

ANALOGIES

Like metaphors and stories, analogies can give clients a different perspective on their situation and create new ways to behave, think, and act in support of their goals. For example, a client might say, "I keep getting off track with my goals, due to distractions, interruptions, and other things that happen during the week."

The coach could respond, "That is so very normal. What if you saw your life as a journey down a river on a rubber raft? You would naturally come upon some boulder and other obstacles along your journey. But if you are rafting, you would have a helmet, life preserver, and probably even a guide to help you navigate around or over some of the boulders. We all have boulders in our daily lives and they are just part of the journey. How can you begin to find the support you need to avoid certain obstacles, or make sure you have the right equipment and assistance if needed to navigate the others?"

The skills and techniques presented in this chapter are varied and in some cases may blend together. It's like having various types and sizes of tools in a toolbox. Some are hand tools, some are power tools, and some might be turbo-powered. You might need all of them or just one or two. These skills can be used to practice during your transition from therapist or counselor to coach. After using these skills purposefully for a while, they will become second nature for you. But if you ever feel "rusty" or just want to try something different with a client, refer to these as you would a recipe book. Adapt them to your heart's content and have fun as you assist your clients to step into the life they really, really, want.

CHAPTER TEN

Developing and Marketing Your Life Coaching Practice

If not now, when?

—The Talmud

As therapists, we were certainly not taught much about building our business. In fact, we do not even call it a business—we call it a practice! Further, most of us were taught that it was even unethical and unprofessional to market or advertise our services. It was not until the late 1980s that we started to have yellow-page ads with descriptions of our services, and you certainly never mentioned in conversations at cocktail parties that you could help someone with their problem. As a coach you are a businessperson providing a unique form of assistance. You can speak about it, advertise it, and enthusiastically let people know you might be able to help them reach their goals. You can even meet in public to discuss how your services might be of use.

Obviously, a crucial component for your transition to coaching is learning entrepreneurial skills and the simple and powerful development and marketing steps for a successful business. It's only natural for most helping professionals to be uncomfortable with the idea of marketing or selling. In this chapter we will show you new ways to approach marketing as a way of letting people know what you do.

Marketing versus Selling

Most of us often confuse marketing with selling. We probably hear ourselves saying things like:

"I don't like selling."
"I can't take rejection."
"Selling is unprofessional."
"I do not want to appear pushy."
"I became a therapist, not a salesperson."

We understand these fears. They come from your inner gremlin or your self-critic. But there are many ways to market your business and to see marketing as something enjoyable and natural. Think of it this way. If you are right-handed and lost the use of your right hand, you could eventually become proficient and comfortable using your left hand. It just takes practice and a willingness to change.

We also believe that the marketing methods you use should be enjoyable (although they may take some practice to achieve a good comfort level). Remember that you are not knocking on doors or telemarketing to sell a product that people do not want. Most people will want coaching. The goal is to attract the type of client you want to work with and for whom your services are both valuable and affordable. Isn't that true for the professional services you utilize?

Stop Being a Secret!

Our basic philosophy is that if you want people to hire you as a coach, you must stop "being a secret." The principle of attracting clients is more powerful than the manipulative promotion and selling of other sales professionals, but if you are going to follow the principle of attraction, remember that the word "action" comprises more than half of the word. You will not get clients by just wishing and hoping they will contact you. They need to know that you exist, what it is you do, and the benefits they (or those they might refer) might receive by working with you as a coach.

As we have trained helping professionals to become coaches, we have heard many people talk about their beliefs, myths, and misconceptions about marketing. Our training approach is based on five key principles.

1. Marketing is *not* selling. We wish we had thought of it first, but as Peter Drucker, the business and management consultant, said so eloquently: "The purpose of marketing is to make selling unnecessary (1973)." We definitely agree. Of course, technically, you are selling. You are selling your self and your service, but it should be done in a way that does not feel or look like selling. However, you need to learn to market until your business grows to the point of being filled mostly by referrals—the ideal position for a self-sustaining business.

2. Therapists have the necessary marketing skills because we are trained to listen well, communicate clearly, and are good at creating relationships. This is why marketing gurus of today, especially in service-oriented businesses, say that networking is the key to business success. What is networking? It is developing relationships with people so they can know what it is you do and you know what it is they do. Networking is the way business is built through cross-referrals or as a way of serving your clients. Coaches who become master networkers, and can refer their clients to other professionals or services that could assist specific concerns, will have a thriving business and a reputation as someone who knows who to call or where to go. C. J. Hayden (1999) says, "Marketing is telling people what you do... over and over" (p. 5). So, the keys to success as a new coach come from figuring out what you want to say about your coaching, how to say it, and to whom you want to say it. If you really love what you do, people will experience your authenticity; even if they don't want to hire you as a coach, they may know someone who will. In coaching, you are hired more for *who you are* than for the specifics of *what you do*. If you are enjoying your life and coach people so that they can too, you are very attractive as a coach. People want some of what you have. They will want you to help them achieve the level of happiness and clarity of vision that you have. All you need to do is guide them to achieve or develop their life according to their desired agenda.

3. Marketing your practice successfully and easily is more likely to occur when you clarify what you do, how you do it, who you work best with, etc. Clarity allows you to focus your efforts, your resources, and your energies. It also allows you to craft a message about your coaching busi-

ness that will attract clients to you (if you are not a secret). Clarity allows you to create a *fulfilling* practice as distinct from a *full* practice. We will say more about this later.

4. Marketing your coaching business successfully can happen only when you have created the space and time and energy for this new business paradigm to occur.

5. Be a resource. As you get to know other coaches, professionals, and books and places where your clients can go for specific help or services, you become increasingly valuable. Keep a good database of international professionals, coaches, and schools. You can often find some helpful direction or resource for your client with a quick phone call or e-mail. This is impressive as you become more than just a coach. And it doesn't take much time or energy if you have the resources and contacts readily available.*

Marketing Your Practice

In the early stages of developing your coaching business, you can start by getting some business cards, creating client folders, and being ready for your first "customer." We will discuss the logistics and pragmatics of setting up your business in the next section. For now, when you are ready to start coaching (and we hope you have had some formal training beyond reading this book), you need to start trying on the metaphoric coach's uniform. Get accustomed to using the words *life coach, personal coach,* or *business coach.* The popularity of coaching makes marketing much easier than it used to be. We cannot stress enough, however, that although you may be able to add coaching to your business and learn much from this book and others, you are not likely to become a master life coach without some formal coach-specific training and consulting with your own personal coach. (See the information about coach-training programs in the Resources.)

Developing a Target Niche

The current wisdom in marketing today, especially for a service-oriented business, is to develop one to three target niches. As a therapist or counselor,

---

*We are grateful to the work of Diane Menendez, Ph.D. for many of the ideas in this chapter. Diane is the curriculum developer and lead instructor for the Institute for Life Coach Training. She also assisted in the design of this content by Patrick Williams and Sherry Lowry, the original developers of the Life Coach Training Program of TherapistU, which is now the Institute for Life Coach Training.

you may have some special expertise or skills that would lend themselves to a specific niche. For example, if you already do marriage or couples counseling, you could market yourself as a relationship coach. We know many relationship coaches who do couples coaching by phone and attract busy, dual-income couples who want to improve their relationships and often just need the space and time devoted to coaching for transformation to occur.

Another possible niche would be family business coaching for a skilled systems-oriented therapist who is knowledgeable about the unique dynamics that arise in family-owned businesses. There are also associations and specific training available, for those who would like to be known as specializing in coaching family businesses. Teen coaching, family coaching, coaching people with ADD, etc., are other obvious niches for skilled therapists.

We know a former career counselor who now has a full-time coaching business and her niche is career coaching. All she really needed to change was the way she described her business. She still gives traditional assessments and job-search "coaching," but now she can do it internationally through faxes and e-mails. When clients complete their career-specific coaching, they often want to retain her as their life coach; the coaching then takes on a more whole-life perspective.

A way to develop a possible niche is to take a look at who comes into your office now. What kinds of clients are you best with? Who you enjoy working with the most? However, many therapists-turned-coaches develop new interests and may not want to do the same type of coaching as the therapy they did. It may also be confusing as to whether you are attracting coachable clients or clients who need therapeutic interventions. This can be one of the most challenging areas in your transition. Confer with your own coach or mentor about this.

Branding versus Niche Development

We have had discussions with many of our trainees in our coach-training business, or with therapists we have mentored to become coaches, about the distinction between branding and niche development.

Branding is based on the concept of singularity. It creates in the mind of the prospect the perception that there is no product on the market quite like your product (Ries & Ries, 1998, p. 7). You are your product. The coaching service you provide is your coaching—your style, your personality, your energy, your insight, and your integrity. Branding as a coach implies that you consider your own unique qualities and the unique qualities of the persons you really want to coach, and you then give that combination a brand. For example, Pat is known for his Total Life Coaching™ and Total Life Creation™ approaches to life coaching. Deb is known for Human Dynamics.

One coach that we know wants to be known as the "life balance coach" and works with "busy professionals on the go who want to achieve balance in work, family, and fun." That is an example of a branding more than a niche. Next, she might think of a niche market where she could find such busy professionals, i.e., lawyers, therapists, entrepreneurs, etc. Can you see how this could be her entrée into coaching? How do you want to be branded?

TRY IT!

Ask three friends and three colleagues what they find unique about you and your relationship with them. What do they get from you that is special? You are as unique as a snowflake or fingerprint. How does that impact who you coach and how you coach? How might this lead to a *brand?* Write down your thoughts and feedback in your coaching notebook or journal.

No Matter Where You Go, There You Are

Marketing can occur all the time because as a therapist (and as a coach) it is you that people hire, and the *you* that you present in public is part of the marketing. Another way to say this is that *you are your message.* This does not mean you are always selling, but it does mean that informal ways of meeting people or having conversations will eventually lead to the ubiquitous question, "What do you do?" How you answer that or how you even get that question to be asked of you is the simplest, most efficient way to market your coaching business. We and many of our colleagues have actually found clients at the local tennis club, at an informal networking meeting, or on an airplane ride. The latter is actually more common than you think! How many times have you conversed with your seatmate on a plane and asked them, "What do you do?" If you ask it of them, they will ask it of you. One of the rules of good networking is to be interested in other people. People love to talk about themselves and if you are genuinely interested in them and what their business is, or what their hobbies are, or what dreams they have, then they will most likely ask you what you do—bingo! You could have a potential client.

Another marketing tip is often called the "elevator speech" or "magic moment." It is a quick response for those inevitable times when someone asks, "What do you do?" We like to refer to it as your *laser intro!* A laser intro, as its name suggests, is done quickly and gets right to the point. The point is to let people know what you do, so that they might ask more questions about how you do what you do. That then leads to further conversation or at a future time where you get to give the details about how you work as a life coach and how you might be able to help them. There are six key components of an effective laser intro or elevator speech:

1. Is it *clear?* Your response to "What do you do?" must be clear, free of jargon, easily understood.
2. Is it *concise?* A laser intro should be brief and delivered in 15 seconds or less.
3. Is it *compelling* or *captivating?* Your message must have a compelling quality, one that begs further inquiry, and peaks the interest of the listener.
4. Is it *conversational?* Your message should be delivered in an informal manner. This takes practice. You must be so natural and automatic with your message that it does not sound like a rehearsed speech. A conversationally delivered message will encourage further conversation to your audience.
5. Is it delivered with *confidence?* The more practiced and natural you are, the more confident and passionate you are about what you do, the more attractive your message is. Remember that you are your message.
6. Is the word *coach* in your message? Somewhere in your message you must say you are a coach (life coach, business coach, personal coach, relationship coach, parent coach, etc.). It is important for you to provide details about your style of coaching so that the listener can judge whether he or she would like your services.

Having two or three laser intros is important so that you can adapt the basic message to your audience while still describing very quickly what you do. Here are a few tried-and-true laser intros we and other coaches have used successfully.

Q: What do you do?
A: I am a personal life coach. You know how people often have that gap

between where they are and where they want to be? I work with them on filling the gap and creating the life they really want.

Q: What is it that you do?
A: Pretty much anything I want on any given day! And I teach others to do it too! Does that sound like something that might interest you?

Q: What do you do?
A: I am a personal life coach. You know how a plumber comes in and snakes out your pipes to get the water flowing freely? What I do is work with people to unclog the personal and business blocks that keep their lives from flowing freely.

After the laser intro gets attention, hopefully the person might ask something like, "That sounds interesting. . . . How do you do that?" Then the door is open to set a meeting over coffee, or better yet, grant him or her a free 30-minute coaching call so he or she can experience it firsthand. Even if you do not gain a client, he or she will at the very least know of your style and may become a great referral source for you!

In fact, your goal when you network with people or dialogue about your careers is to be open to the possibility that the person may be really interested in what you do and want to know more. It is at this opportunity that we recommend being a living brochure*—don't just talk about what coaching is, demonstrate it. Ask if you can coach the person on something they want to change or some long-term goal. A spot coaching demonstration gives potential clients a taste of coaching and they may want the entire menu!

Now that you have a good idea of how you can market your business and build your coaching visibility, it is very helpful to know some key strategies for your actual marketing plan. You may know what to say and how to say it, but you need people to hear it. Generally speaking, Yellow Page ads and other traditional advertising methods do not work in this person-centered business. You need to speak with people and network in ways that increase your visibility and expand your geographical market. Remember, in a tele-coaching business, you are not geographically bound. Like many coaches, we have international practices, so the whole world is literally your target market!

---

*This term comes from Robert Alderman, a longtime coach and mentor.

Helpful Marketing Ideas

Here are 50 tips from Rich Fettke, an early pioneer in coaching and one of the leaders of the International Coach Federation. His ideas are food for thought as you begin to contemplate how you want to market your coaching business.

50 Great Marketing Ideas for Coaches*
How to Climb to the Top!

You are on the way to climbing the magnificent mountain named . . . Your Career! To get to the top depends largely on how well you market yourself. Below are 50 great ways to help you reach higher levels of success. Remember, you can do any of these, but please don't try to do all of them. This large list of ideas is not intended to have you get overwhelmed. Choose a few strategies and focus on doing them well. See how they work and then keep what works best for you . . . then try a few more.

Make sure you have a great coach to work with on your path. A coach is like a professional climbing partner, who will help guide, support and encourage you. The journey will be more enjoyable, and you will be far more apt to succeed. No climber would attempt to conquer a mountain alone. Why try to attain mountain-size goals alone? Having a coach is vital to your success. If you were climbing a mountain you might find yourself stuck, fearful, discouraged, or exhausted. Your climbing partner, just like your coach, would help you see your next move, keep you focused, bring you back to your original purpose, and cheer you on to success.

If you have ideas that have worked for you on your path to success, please share them with me and I will share them with others. That's a win-win for everyone. Here are 50 marketing ideas for your success. I wish you the best as you climb to the top with clarity and focus. Enjoy the journey and reach high!

*Copyright 2001 by Rich Fettke. The original source of this material is Rich Fettke, MCC, speaker, coach, and author of *Extreme Success*. www.Fettke.com.

1. **Create a Unique Marketing Message**—Your Unique Marketing Message is a short, 30-second sound bite that tells people what you do and what makes you unique. Your Unique Marketing Message should always offer benefits.

2. **Create a Promo Kit**—This is a high-quality folder you can give or mail to prospects and the media that contains all or some of the following: your photo, articles you've written, articles written about you, your brochure, your resume, a list of questions you are frequently asked and the answers to those questions, your vision, your mission, your audio tape, and anything else that lets people know who you are and how you can help them.

3. **Use Your Photo . . . Everywhere**—People remember faces, not always names. If you use your photo on your business cards, your letterhead and your advertising, you will have a better chance of being remembered and people also feel as if they know you better. As you may have heard, successful peoples' names and faces often appear in public places!

4. **Join a Networking Group**—Business networking groups (also called leads groups) are regular meetings where people exchange contacts and referrals. Ask local business people for suggestions on networking groups in your area.

5. **Speak at Local Service Clubs**—A great way to gain credibility and visibility. Rotary clubs, Kiwanis clubs, Lions clubs and Chamber of Commerce meetings are always looking for speakers. Speak on a message you are passionate about and that directly relates to your business. Don't forget to offer handouts with your phone number, email address and web site so your audience can contact you later. Remember, first impressions are very important, so I recommend joining Toastmasters to hone your speaking skills. See #16.

6. **Create an Advocate List**—Begin to notice the people who rave about you. These are your advocates! They may be friends, clients, or associates. They are your best referral resources. Your advocates will send you business simply because they believe in you. Make sure you recognize them. Never let more than 30 days go by without staying in touch with each of your advocates. You can stay in touch with a phone call, a meeting, mailing them a personal note, and of course . . . by sending them business, too.

7. **Write Articles**—When your work is published in a magazine, newsletter, newspaper you gain credibility and visibility. Always try to have your contact information included in your article. You can later mail copies of your article to your mailing list and include it in your promo kit.

8. **Give Away Free Specialty Gifts**—Give away free specialty gifts with your business name, logo, phone number and web site imprinted on them.

9. **Serve on an Association Committee or Board**—Serving on a committee or board of an association related to your career can help you meet key people in your industry, improve your professional recognition, teach you new leadership skills, and position you in front of possible prospects. It's also a great way to give back to your profession. Most associations are looking for volunteers. Just contact the director or a board member of the association to find out how you might serve.

10. **Give Free or Low-Cost Workshops**—By offering workshops on coaching related topics, such as time management, building a business, living a more balanced life, or goal setting, you can develop your message, meet new prospects, position yourself as an expert and attract new clients. Have an evaluation form for participants to fill out after the workshop with a place for them to fill out their name, address, phone number, email address, etc. You may also want to have a check box that says, "Contact me about Coaching."

11. **Hold a Coaching Evening**—an event for your clients, prospective clients and their friends. You offer a meal or snacks and an interactive talk on a coaching related topic (see #10). Your guests get to meet new people, learn valuable information and see live coaching by a wonderful coach . . . you!

12. **Make an Audio Tape Interview**—Rent time at a recording studio and have a friend (with a good voice) interview you about your business. Have a list of questions already printed up for your interviewer. Then edit the tape, add some music, make duplications and ta-da . . . you have an informative audio tape that you can give or mail to prospects!

13. **Make Quote Cards**—These are business card size "mini posters" with your favorite quotes on them. People love them and will hold on to them for a long time. On the back of the quote card add your name, your company name, your web site address and your contact information. Again, this is just another way to improve your visibility, credibility, and contribution with others.

14. **Have Stories Published About You**—Have someone write a story about you and your business (or do it yourself). Find a newspaper or magazine that is willing to publish your story. Having a press kit helps!

15. **Host Your Own Radio Show**—Many radio stations will allow you to have your own radio show if you pay for the time. You can pay for the time by getting businesses to sponsor your program by buying advertising time during your show. You can interview these business owners, expert guests, and have people call in. Remember to ask for your program to be tape recorded so you can mail tapes to future prospects.

16. **Join Toastmasters**—This is a worldwide organization that has speaking clubs in most cities. Most clubs meet on a weekly basis and the members practice their public speaking skills in front of their club. You can meet new people, find clients, and get referrals from your fellow members. You also get to practice the speeches that you later give to other groups (see #5).

17. **Be Quoted in the Media**—Contact the media and tell them your expertise. Tell them that you are willing to be a resource if they are ever writing a story on your special area. Stay in touch with your contacts at the media offices and in time you may get a call for a quote or interview. These quotes give you credibility and visibility. Make copies of these articles for your promo kit (see #2).

18. **Create Your Ultimate Client Profile**—Make a list of the top 7–10 qualities you look for in a great client. Place this list somewhere you can see it throughout the day. Only accept clients who fit this profile! If someone does not fit, refer him or her to another coach. This takes courage and faith, but you will discover that you will attract the clients you truly love to work with. Your phone will begin to ring and those great prospects will become great clients.

19. **Mail an Introduction Letter**—Send a letter out to your mailing list, friends, and business contacts that explain what you do and how you do it. You may also want to include a gift certificate for a free sample session that they can use or give to their friends.

20. **Display Your Business Cards**—Ask businesses in your area if you can display your business cards and/or brochures. Many businesses will let you do this and it is a very low cost and effective way to get your name out there.

21. **Use the Classified Ads**—This is a low-cost way to advertise on a regular basis. You may want to offer a free session, article or product to people who contact you. Classifieds are also an easy way to promote your web site.

22. **Host Your Own Cable TV Show**—Most local cable television stations offer free studio time to residents. In most cases, you just need to submit a proposal. If you create an entertaining and informative show, they may air it all over your area. Also find out if you can be a guest on someone else's cable show.

23. **Ask Your Clients for Referrals**—You've heard this before but are you doing it? Asking, "Who do you know that might benefit from my services?" is a simple, yet powerful way to meet new prospects. Let your clients know that you are expanding your practice and ask them if they know of anyone to whom you could offer a sample session.

24. **Publish a Newsletter**—Offer valuable information to your readers and your newsletter will be appreciated, read and passed along. A newsletter establishes you as an expert, allows you to keep connected with many people and it gives you a place to share the benefits of working with you.

25. **Donate Your Services to Charity Fund-raisers**—This is often overlooked. Charity fund-raisers that have raffles and auctions are a great place for you to give back and receive recognition at the same time. Most fund-raising groups will include your company name, address, phone number and web site in the materials in exchange for you donation. Ask your local Chamber of Commerce about fund-raisers in your area that are looking for support through donations.

26. **Host a Fund-raising Event**—This is a way to give back even more to your community and meet some wonderful people at the same time. You could organize a race, a workshop, a raffle . . . just about anything you can think of to raise money for a good cause. You not only give back, but you also create more awareness about your company. Givers gain!

27. **Send Press Releases to the Media**—A press release is a great way to get an interview with the print, radio and TV media. Make sure your press release follows the proper format (see books at the library on how to make a press release). Follow up with phone calls and ask if your press release was received and if you can answer any questions. Stay in touch with editors or reporters and let them know that you are a resource if they ever need information related to your expertise.

28. **Offer an On-line Newsletter**—An on-line newsletter via email is a wonderful way to give value to people, share your knowledge, spotlight your expertise and promote your business. Don't expect immediate return on your investment. What you can expect is that people get to know who you are and may eventually use your services. Be sure to ask first if they want to subscribe.

29. **Write a Book**—A book is one of the best ways to increase your visibility and credibility. You don't have to write a 500 page text to be an author. You can start by writing about your experience or expertise, or something you are passionate about. Self-publishing a small, informative booklet is a simple way to get started. Make sure that you include your contact information in the book so readers easily know how to reach you.

30. **Speak at Conferences**—Conferences allow you to share your experience and knowledge with others in related fields. Some conferences pay for speakers while some conferences ask you to volunteer your time. Either way, conferences help you meet prospects and make contacts that can lead to more business for you in the future. Remember to have a short, quality handout for the participants at your program and include your contact information. Conferences are not a place to self-promote; they are a place to share your knowledge. Do this and you will attract business with ease.

31. **Assist at Others' Workshops**—Offer to assist at workshops that you have attended and enjoyed. You not only deepen your learning by hearing the information again, but you also may meet some prospects who want to implement the information they are learning. Make sure your focus is on giving value and the business will attract to you with ease. Bring plenty of business cards!

32. **Create Referral Partnerships**—Find out who may be able to refer their clients, friends or contacts to you. Look for people you believe in, so that you can do the same for them. For example, an accountant may refer a new business owner to you to help her stay focused and on track as she grows her business. You may refer one of your clients to the accountant so they can more wisely manage their money. This is a win-win for everyone!

33. **Speak at Book Stores**—Ask a local book store owner if you can speak on your area of expertise. Tell him that you will be suggesting several books that he sells during your presentation. When you give your program, inform the audience of how working with you will help them put the ideas from the book into action.

34. **Join your Chamber of Commerce**—Your local Chamber of Commerce is an invaluable source of leads and referral partners. You may also be able to write articles for their newsletters and give workshops to fellow members on your area of expertise.

35. **Attend Workshops**—Simply attending workshops to enhance your personal/professional development is a way to market your business. You will find yourself surrounded by people who are interested in learning and growing—perfect candidates for coaching!

36. **Use Postcards**—Postcards are a cost-effective way to stay in touch with prospects, clients and referral sources. Develop a theme or character that people will recognize over time. Send out postcards with article quotes, testimonials, opinion surveys, correspondence, reminders, thank you's, announcements, newsletters, or just to say "hello." If you've published a book, duplicate the cover of the book onto a postcard and it becomes an advertising piece. Create a postcard that is a one-sheet flyer to hand out when people ask for information. Remember . . . marketing is telling people what you do over and over again!

37. **Create a Mastermind Group**—Meet with 3-5 friends or colleagues on a regular basis to discuss each of your goals, plans and dreams. When a group of people come together, new ideas are created that might not have been discovered alone. (We know this to be true as coaches!) Together you will brainstorm new ways to market yourselves and also hold each other accountable. Everyone wins in a mastermind group!

38. **Serve on a Panel**—Serving on a panel at a conference or meeting gives you credibility and visibility. Associations in your area may be looking for an expert to speak about the benefits of coaching. Contact them, ask them if they need panelists for future programs, tell them what you offer, and let them know you are a willing resource.

39. **Have a Comprehensive Set of Client Handouts**—Have a variety of exercises, handouts and give-aways that describe your practice, solve problems, and provide value for your clients. Make sure to give all of your clients useful tools, information and ideas to share with their friends.

40. **Contact Former Clients**—Many coaches forget that former clients may be interested in coaching again or that they can be great sources of information and referrals. Often they are at a new place in their lives and they are ready for change and new growth. I challenge you to contact three of your former clients this week! Show interest; find out how they are doing. Let them know they are the most important part of your research and development program. Listen to their suggestions. Make it a normal part of your service to follow-up with your former clients every two to three months.

41. **Join the International Coach Federation (ICF)**—The ICF is the primary worldwide resource for business and personal coaches and is a great resource for those who are seeking a coach. The ICF is an individual membership organization formed by professionals worldwide who practice and/or teach business and personal coaching. The ICF provides many resources, and can help you meet other coaches, prospects and leaders. The ICF also holds an annual conference where you can learn new marketing skills and tools. Call the ICF at 888-423-3131 or visit their web site at www.coachfederation.org.

42. **List yourself on the ICF's Coach Referral Service**—The ICF maintains high visibility for the profession through public relations, publicity campaigns, marketing strategies and the Coach Referral Service (CRS). The CRS is the only recognized independent system that matches coaches with clients seeking their services. This system is accessible both on the internet and by phone. Hundreds of coaches worldwide list their practice and even link their home page. The CRS receives broad media coverage and is generating an ever-increasing amount of visibility for members.

43. **Have a Web Site**—A web site alone is just a tool, not a complete strategy. You must let people know your site is there for it to have impact. Also, give your visitors valuable information on your site and think of ways to have them come back for more. To get the most visibility for your site list it at the end of your email messages, give the site's address on your outgoing voice mail message, put it on your business card, letterhead, postcards, etc. A web site is also very helpful when someone calls you for information. Instead of having to mail out flyers and brochures, you can give your web site address. Your prospects will have your information in front of them almost instantly!

44. **Create a Marketing Plan**—Include a description of your specific client populations and your plans for reaching them. Include budgets for your time energy and the money to implement your plan. If potential clients don't know about you, or can't find you, they won't hire you. Choose a few items on this list and build them into your plan. Set goals and then track your results. Look at other coaches who are successful. What have they done to achieve that success? Focus on what works for you as an individual and then commit to your plan with action and passion!

45. **Model a Great Life**—A healthy, balanced, successful life is extremely attractive! Be an example of someone who is living a great life. Surround yourself with delightful, challenging and exciting people. Notice where you can improve areas of your life, such as relationships, fitness, playtime, finances, and your personal integrity. Then hire your own coach to support you in taking action! If you "walk your talk," people will notice and you will begin to attract new clients with ease.

46. **Form "Combo" Alliances**—Form an alliance with your suppliers, colleagues or even competitors to offer a "combo" package that neither of you could offer alone. This way you will share the marketing expenses. Attorneys and accountants can offer compelling packages. For example: A life coach might form an alliance with a gym, weight-loss or stop-smoking program.

47. **Use Your Outgoing Voice-Mail Message**—Don't overlook this simple, yet effective way to promote your services. Let your callers know what you do and the benefits you offer. Remember to give them a way (right up front) to by-pass your message if they don't want to listen to the whole thing. If you are using a digital voice mail service, you may want to have different voice mail boxes and outgoing messages for each service you offer.

48. **"Claim" a Client**—Claiming is a very special way to have someone become your client. You can "claim" them, just as you would stake a claim on something you really want. Let them know that they are the type of client you love to work with, that you believe in their goals, work with them as their coach. Tell them that you won't take no for an answer, and that you are willing to do whatever it takes. Don't use this as a sales technique because people have built in lie detectors. They will know if you are being insincere. "Claiming" must be authentic and come straight from the heart.

49. **Offer Free Things to People**—If you write an article, have a web site, or get interviewed on television or radio, it's a good idea to offer a free giveaway to your audience. You not only strengthen your relationship with them but you can also add them to your mailing list for future contact. This giveaway might be a free report like the one you are reading right now. Giver's gain!

50. **Care about People!**—This is the most important step of all. No prior steps will work without this one. As you may have heard, people don't care what you know until they know you care. With any marketing strategy, offer your benefits and services first.

As we said earlier, most of us were not taught business or marketing skills and we do not like to see ourselves as salespeople. It has been said that opening a relationship is the first step to closing the sale. Marketing your coaching business requires relationship marketing and networking as ways for you to *stop being invisible*. Have fun, and work with a mentor coach who has made the transition from therapy to coaching successfully.

Part IV
Expanding Your Coaching Practice

CHAPTER ELEVEN

Broadening Your Base: Beyond Basic Life Coaching

Ain't no man that can avoid being born average, but ain't nobody got to be common.

—Satchel Paige

The advent of telecoaching and the Internet has erased geographical barriers and enabled you to have an international coaching business from your home or portable office. This not only expands your market globally but also creates ways in which you can go beyond the traditional one-on-one coaching model. As a therapist or counselor, you may have found group therapy to be efficient and financially rewarding. The client got more impact for less money and you, as the leader, got a higher hourly fee. The same wisdom holds true for group coaching, and you do not have to limit yourself to in-person groups at your office location. Group coaching can be done by telephone with clients in various states and countries.

There are three unique ways to incorporate group coaching into your practice, whether you do live groups or groups over the telephone.*

1. Group coaching as added value with existing clients
2. Group coaching with a specific market niche (e.g., managers of various branch offices, entrepreneurs in similar businesses, franchise owners from different locales)

---

*For phone groups you will have to rent or own a bridge line. This is a phone number that is reserved exclusively for participants to call and be on the phone at the same time without the hassle of using an operator. See the Resources for more information.

3. Group coaching using a personal development book as the tool for discussion and exploration

We will now give practical examples of these.

Group Coaching as Added Value

Many life coaches offer group coaching as an added value for paying clients. For example, you could have a group phone call (also called teleconferencing) once a month for all clients to present a coaching goal or a personal or professional challenge. It is a great way to have your clients get to know one another; this can create mastermind thinking that is synergistic. Just like in group therapy, when one person receives coaching on a particular challenge or desire, others most likely will benefit by listening for similar challenges in their own lives. Some coaches have scheduled group calls as a Saturday Clean the Clutter Day—almost every person de-clutters their office, garage, or closets together. This can make de-cluttering a fun and interactive way for your clients to create more space in their lives and gain energy.

Other group calls with existing clients can be about any similar theme that comes up for all of them; the call could be a conversation about marketing or about balancing work and life. These group calls are easy for you to facilitate and they will become your best marketing tool as clients shout your praises to their colleagues and friends. We recommend you conduct these groups free of charge for existing clients for this reason alone.

Group Coaching with a Specific Market Niche

Many coaches have found it very lucrative to expand their practice into some group coaching with specific niches after they have gained experience and visibility in the coaching field. An example of using group coaching in this way would be to offer group coaching twice a month for one hour or so, with local business owners. You can easily find them through your chamber of commerce. As a coach you can be very helpful to new entrepreneurs who need to stay focused on the steps that will help them be more successful. You are not a business consultant here—just a business coach (or life coach), helping them articulate what they want and what is needed to help them succeed. This is an old-fashioned support group, but with people who presumably do not have mental or emotional disorders. It is a coaching group, not a therapy group, even though support is one of the benefits it offers.

When Pat started his full-time coaching career, he connected with The Center for Business Development at a local community college and proposed the idea of doing group coaching with CEOs of small businesses who could not afford to have their own board of directors. He formed a group of non-competing small-business CEOs who met initially for a one-day, in-person seminar on business coaching; they then participated in a bimonthly one-hour conference call to create sustainable results over time with major goals for their companies. There are groups such as The Young Presidents, TEC (The Executive Committee), or TAB (The Alternative Board), which are set up to be very exclusive with a trained facilitator (coach) for a very high fee, and they combine in-person meetings with coaching sessions between meetings. Pat designed a group called The Sounding Board™ in which eight CEOs confer during two phone calls a month and half-day in-person meetings four times a year.

Think of the various groups that could benefit from group coaching. What about owners of the same franchise in various parts of the country, such as owners of MailBoxes Etc. franchises? Couldn't they benefit from a coaching group composed of people trying to build the same business? Of course, they get some mentoring/training from the corporate headquarters, but they often do not get to connect with other franchise owners in a less formal, regular way. Keep in mind that group coaching is not "telling people" how to run their businesses. They have rules, policies, and regular procedures from their corporate headquarters. Coaching is to help them be more focused, more innovative, and more fulfilled in the way they run their life and their business.

Group Coaching with a Personal Development Book

This is an exciting area of coaching and one that is becoming more and more popular. Remember, with the use of a teleconference line, you can attract clients from any geographical area and create a very rich and stimulating atmosphere for like-minded persons who are exploring similar personal goals. We do not believe in reinventing the wheel; you do not need to develop unique or new programs or curricula if you do not want to—use an existing book or program. If all participants buy the book, it will be a common background and map for the group. And you are not plagiarizing anything, because you require that each participant buy the book you are using as the guide for the group.

Here are books that lend themselves well to a group-coaching format. Your groups can be time-limited (e.g., for twelve weeks, six months, etc.) or they can be ongoing with people joining as spaces open and picking up from there).

Take Time for Your Life and/or *Life Makeovers* by Cheryl Richardson. These books are both best-sellers and very popular because they have practical, doable strategies. Having a coach to walk participants through the assignments is often critical. Reading a good book is not the same as doing what it suggests. Remember that a lot of "self-help" books become "shelf help," resting on bookshelves having never been used or read completely.

The Portable Coach: 28 Surefire Strategies for Business and Personal Success by Thomas Leonard. This book is very easily adapted to a group discussion format and can be delivered as a sequential guide, presented in chapter order. Or it can be used as a just-in-time (in the moment) coaching model for asking the group which of the 28 principles were a success or a challenge in their lives that week. Then the coaching begins!

Falling Awake: Creating the Life of Your Dreams by Dave Ellis. This book is jam-packed with dozens of ways to create a more fulfilling life and includes 12 success strategies.

Divine Intuition: Your Guide to Creating a Life You Love by Lynn A. Robinson, M.Ed. Cheryl Richardson said in the foreword, "Lynn combines spiritual wisdom with practical advice to help you discover your best path to a life you love."

Life Strategies: Doing What Works, Doing What Matters by Phil McGraw. Phil is a popular "coach" on Oprah and calls himself a life strategist. He is also a psychologist and this book is a commonsense and practical guide that can be a useful resource for group coaching.

The Artist's Way by Julia Cameron. This has been used effectively by both therapists and coaches. It encourages the use of a personal journal and has creative tasks geared toward spontaneity and play and looking at living as an art form. This book links spiritual development to creativity by showing how to connect with the creative energies of the universe. Since its publication in the mid-nineties, it has spawned a remarkable number of support groups for artists and nonartists dedicated to practicing its prescriptions and exercises. It is a great springboard for a coaching group.

Specialties in Coaching

The history of coaching (discussed in chapter 2) revealed that its main use was in the corporate environment via executive coaching. The following subsections will highlight various new niches or special applications of coaching beginning with executive and corporate coaching. You will also read about the very creative approaches of some therapists who have transitioned successfully to coaching in these niches. Our hope is that you may find one of these specialties excites you, and you can contact the coach for more information about their approach. Or you may get a creative idea applying coaching in a way that is not mentioned here. In the future there will not only be coaches in private practice, but coaches in high schools, churches, probation departments, etc. so the range of coaching niches will be limitless.

Executive and Corporate Coaching

This is where it all began. Coaching for executives and top-level managers has been around since the seventies, but it dramatically increased in popularity in the latter half of the twentieth century and seems poised for tremendous growth as corporations become more "intrapreneurial" for the new millennium. For companies to stay on the leading edge and keep the best top executives, many companies either hire outside coaches for both training and coaching or train their managers to function more as coaches than supervisors. Leadership development and mentoring of younger employees is also a common use of coaches today. In fact, there is also "reverse mentoring" wherein younger employees are taught to coach older employees on subjects like technology so that older employees do not have to feel "behind the times."

Executive and corporate coaching can be very lucrative as it benefits the client company with decreased turnover, more effective management, creation of new products and services, and happier employees, all of which increase company's profit and growth. This is a continuously dynamic opportunity for the coach who is comfortable and savvy in the corporate arena. Ideally an executive or corporate coach should have a graduate degree or work experience in business, human resources, or organizational development, coupled with specialized coach training for a corporate environment.

Retirement Coaching

For many people, retirement means quitting a job for good, utilizing pension and savings, moving to warmer climates or the place they always wanted to live, or spending time playing golf, fishing, and traveling. Isn't that the American dream? Today, due to inheritance, investments, and increased affluence, many professionals are retiring earlier. And, within the next few years, the cavalcade of baby boomers approaching retirement age increases exponentially. It is baby boomers who hire personal coaches for the most part, so it makes sense that retirement coaching will become a niche or specialty area, sooner than later. In fact, we prefer to call this niche protirement coaching (Hudson, 1999). Protirement, in our view, sounds similar to what Carl Jung professed that the latter half of life should be: a pursuit of meaning and purpose and a consciousness of what legacy one is leaving to the coming generations (Jung, 1953). Some call this moving from aging to saging—being available to mentor, coach, teach, create, and inspire younger generations.

We believe that protirement coaching can have a powerful impact on the individual and society and is fun for the coach, because these clients have assumedly "already made it," and the coaching is more about legacy and creativity than it is about career, life challenges, or transitions as it is with younger clients. Remember, this is the opportunity for people to be doing exactly what they want to do, whether they need income or not. Protirement is doing your life's work by living a full and fulfilling life.

Coaching International Clients

Many coaches have clients from different countries. That is one of the joys of telephone coaching. There is also a niche in coaching employees of international companies who are sent to foreign countries for extended periods of their lives. That adjustment can sometimes be challenging and having a coach who understands and can help plan for smoothing the experience can be very helpful.

Coaching internationally may also mean coaching foreigners who have a different cultural heritage; you should train for this by learning other languages, personalities and cultural uniqueness. This experience of course can also lead to travel and consulting or training opportunities. There are specialized courses available on international coaching or you could hire a mentor coach who coaches international companies and clients.

Relationship Coaching

One specialty area that will always be popular is relationship coaching. After all, isn't much of marriage and couples work psychoeducational? We believe that many relationships could be helped to be more loving, more purposeful, and more satisfying if couples understood that having a coach can be occasionally helpful, even when the relationship is not in trouble. Haven't we always hoped couples would access couples counseling before struggling with their relationships?

Relationship coaching has more appeal than couples counseling (especially to men) and does not carry a stigma; it can be viewed as a skill-building, stress-reducing service. Therefore, we believe that more couples will seek it as it becomes more available and publicized. There will, of course, still be couples who do need more intense therapy, but many couples (and singles) simply need regular scheduled visits with a relationship coach in order to be taught and guided on how to hold open dialogues.

Many life coaches will refer their clients to relationship coaches for specialized work. Relationship coaching can be utilized even when either of the partners has another coach for business or personal life goals. We both, and many coaches we know, refer clients to short-term relationship coaching as part of their clients' overall life plans. Many busy coaches also hire their own relationship coach because they know how easy it is to lose focus on having the most loving and joyful relationship possible. Relationship coaching could become available and utilized as one would other "maintenance programs" in one's life. Why not have an annual relationship checkup and then get tune-ups as needed?

One of our colleagues, David Steele (who can be reached at www.life partnerquest.com), has even built a niche specializing in coaching singles and teaching counselors and coaches how to work with singles. He believes it is valuable and important to coach singles on how to find the right relationship and then how to maintain that relationship in a healthy fashion. Relationship coaching and singles coaching is really coaching, teaching, and guiding all wrapped into one. Consider how many couples now both work amid great stress and less time, and you will see a potentially big and positive niche for coaches. Therapists trained in *Imago* (Hendrix, 1988) or John Gottman's work (1976, 1994, 1999), or Michele Weiner-Davis's *Divorce Busting* (1992) and others can easily transition those techniques and strategies into coaching couples. Relationship coaching helps couples have outstanding relationships, not mediocre ones.

Coaching Students

Several of our colleagues coach students in regard to adjustment or applying to college, life or career planning, or life in general. Many parents are happy to pay for their children to have a coach and, again, there is no stigma as there sometimes is with having a therapist. Other coaches work within a school setting; for example, one coach we know has developed coaching groups in her college counseling center focusing on career planning, relationships, or anything else that students want to explore.

Another colleague coaches students with special needs through her community college office providing support to individuals with psychological or neurological disabilities. These students really benefit from the coaching by gaining self-esteem, creative ideas for their lives, and improved relationships and personal responsibility. This coach works to help students learn how to uncover their unique gifts and talents and adapt to their disabilities.

Teen coaching, as a subspecialty of coaching students, is another natural extension of coaching for therapists who have worked with teens in their clinical practices. Teen coaching is for those adolescents who straddle the proverbial fence—being stuck between independent, responsible adulthood and dependent, experimental childhood. Parents and teens are both challenged by the transition in this phase of letting go versus keeping control. Many parents embrace coaching; for fathers and teens, it is an especially positive way to become the best they can, as individuals and family members. Teens, particularly, view coaching as an opportunity to initiate their own path, outside of the immediate scrutiny and volition of their parents. Wouldn't we all have benefited from a formal coaching relationship at some point during our formative years?

Parent/Family Coaching

Another area that seems like a natural transition for therapists-turned-coaches is parent and family coaching. How much of what you do in the areas of parenting classes, child therapy, and family work could be provided under the umbrella of parent and family coaching? Once again, families that have avoided stigma of getting therapy can find the prospect of coaching services more palatable. We know several colleagues who offer special coaching services by in-person groups, workshops, and follow-up family coaching, either face to face or by telephone. Like relationship coaching, parent and family coaching can be presented as short-term, information-rich coaching, it can assist the family to understand the dynamics of healthy family functioning, and it can give them the opportunity to design, create, and dialogue about how they want family life to be. We see this as an incredible opportunity for family coaches and for families in the new millennium when family and parental challenges may become more difficult.

Family Business Coaching

Therapists trained as family practitioners in systemic thinking and strategic approaches will be very valuable to family-owned-business coaches. Family businesses present unique challenges when family dynamics are added to the complexities and pressures of entrepreneurial businesses. Problems can include harmful expectations of family members; family members working in a business by default, not always by choice; personality conflicts over job roles; disagreements over income, etc. We believe that coaches with experience as family therapists bring incredible knowledge and skills to the prospect of working with family-owned businesses that general life coaches cannot always deliver. Also, there are organizations and associations related to family-owned businesses that give family-business coaches opportunities to write, speak, train, and create products that can increase knowledge of this niche in coaching.

Using Assessments in Coaching

Many therapists have been trained in the use of assessments. These can run the gamut of personality assessments, IQ tests, interest testing, and even projective testing (requiring the interpretation of underlying unconscious complexes and personality disorders).

There are many assessments that are useful in coaching that carry no diagnostic labeling and are used primarily in expanding clients' views of personality styles or behavioral tendencies that could help or hinder certain aspects of their lives. The most common coaching assessments are the Myers-Briggs, DISC behavioral assessment and values assessment (both based on early theories of Carl Jung), the Firo-B (Fundamental Interpersonal Relations Orientation Behavior), the 16PF (Sixteen Personality Factor Questionnaire), and the 360-degree assessment (used in corporate and small business coaching) for both individuals and corporate teams or management. One of our colleagues, Mike Lillibridge, has developed The PeopleMap, which is a quick assessment with six different personality types and lends itself extremely well to coaching. (See Resources for information on obtaining these assessments).

Handled by a skillful coach, the results of these assessments can be enlightening and transformational. Handled by a novice or someone untrained in human dynamics, they can be disastrous and wounding. We believe that mental health professionals familiar with group dynamics and communicating assessment data can become strong coaches in this area. We also believe that some advanced training in using assessments may be required in order to use these assessment approaches in the coaching process. These assessments all gather information about tendencies or behaviors that may help a client or corporate team to understand how some strengths in some contexts may be weaknesses in different contexts. Just as one could learn to use one's left hand if it was necessary (if they are naturally right-handed), one can learn to adapt or improve different behaviors or learn where their natural tendencies are best applied. Using assessments in coaching should expand and clarify clients' possibilities for excelling and, when necessary, point out problem areas for learning, training, and coaching.

As you can see, there are many ways that coaching can be applied in special approaches. It is really endless. The examples presented in this chapter are just a few. Use your imagination, work with your coach, and create a way to coach that rekindles your life's passion.

CHAPTER TWELVE

Self-care for Life Coaches

Live with Intention
Walk to the Edge
Listen Hard
Practice Wellness
Play with Abandon
LAUGH
Choose with no regret
Appreciate your friends
Do what you love
Live as if this is all there is
—Maryanne Radmacher-Hershey

Despite all the good qualities of the coaching profession, we have encountered some coaches who are experiencing increasing stress and anxiety, a sense of being "overwhelmed," and frustration with the new work life they have created for themselves. This concerns us. How can life coaches maintain zest and enthusiasm for their work and avoid the burnout that many of us encountered in our previous lives as therapists and other helping professionals? This chapter examines the concept of coach self-care from the holistic perspective of wellness. Burnout is described and coaches' stories we've collected are shared to illustrate what happens when one's life is out of balance. Recommendations from practicing life coaches are offered to guide you as you begin or renew a self-care commitment.

Burnout

Over the past decade, most of us have encountered therapists and other colleagues who we would call "burned-out." Perhaps even you have experienced the realization that it is no longer fun or fulfilling to do the type of helping work that was once the love of your life. Even worse, maybe this feeling became a constant stress on your health and relationships. We wonder how helpers, who are doing so much to improve the human condition, can be in such sad shape themselves? More specifically, why do some life coaches find themselves falling into the same burnout trap that motivated them to leave therapy and other helping professions? Could it be they thought working with a "healthy" population would somehow immunize them to stress-related afflictions? Did they think that setting their own schedule and coaching from home would free them from the overload and frustration they had encountered in their previous line of work? Whatever the reason, we know that believing coaches are invincible to the stresses and toils of other helping professionals is an error, which can be very costly to your wellness and your coaching practice.

Life coaching is not a stress-free practice. If you aren't cautious, you can end up burned-out. However, coach burnout appears to be limited when we consider all the life coaches we know and have mentored. Between us we have mentored over 100 coaches. Coaching as a career seems to energize rather than lead to burnout. The only way burnout occurs with coaches is if they are not working within their own limits and boundaries, which is counterproductive to good coaching. We are unsure if this is simply our isolated experience but speculate that it is related to the unique characteristics of the life coaching profession; the level of experience, preparation, and resilience that therapist-trained coaches bring to a life coaching practice; and the newness of the profession. Clearly, this topic deserves more study and investigation. For the purpose of this book, we believe that a brief review of burnout is important and that a proactive approach to the issue of coach self-care would benefit all of us.

The following stories, shared with us by life coaches describing how they felt about their coaching practices, illustrate coach burnout.

Coach #1

I loved my training and was so thrilled to start my coaching practice. I successfully maintained both part-time therapy and coaching practices for six months. I was good at balancing everything and my practice thrived. It seemed like in no time I had more therapy clients and more coaching clients than I could really handle. Then one of my therapy clients attempted suicide, and I really got behind on my other appointments, both therapy and coaching. Soon it seemed like all I was doing was rescheduling and juggling. A couple of clients left and I stopped working with my mentor coach because I just couldn't find time. Then my daughter got sick, I got sick, and suddenly one day I awoke and realized this wasn't fun any more. Where did I go wrong?

Coach #2

Initially I loved my life coaching practice and was so relieved to be out of therapy and managed care restrictions. Plus, I got to work with healthy individuals on my own terms and schedule. Soon I was traveling, doing some workshops for organizations, and having a lot of fun. I would talk to my clients on the phone at airports and on the road in my car. When I picked up some international clients, I found it increasingly difficult to schedule them into my day and travel like I wanted to across time zones. I originally liked the flexibility of my work but I began to notice that I could never get away from my coaching practice. With therapy, I could at least close the door. This isn't as much fun as it was in the beginning.

These examples of existing or impending burnout are reminders to us that even life coaches, with all their great opportunities and knowledge, must be aware of the signs of burnout. We can implement proactive strategies in our personal and professional lives before burnout becomes a problem. Let's review some of the literature on burnout to determine its applicability to our work as life coaches.

Helping Professional Burnout

Burnout was recognized as a serious cause of impairment among helping professionals in the late 1970s and it is still a matter for concern (Capner & Caltabiano, 1993; Farber, 1990; Figley, 1993; Schaufeli, Maslach, & Marek, 1993). While there is no standard definition of burnout, Freudenberger, considered by many to be the term's originator, described it as "failing, wearing out or becoming exhausted through excessive demands on energy, strength, or resources" (1974, p. 73). Maslach (1982) stated that burnout is "a syndrome of emotional exhaustion, depersonalization and reduced personal accomplishment that can occur among individuals who 'do people work' of some kind" (p. 1). Life coaches certainly face the chronic emotional challenge of dealing intensively with other human beings, particularly when these individuals struggle to find their way and create the lives of their dreams.

Maslach (1982) further identified common threads in the varying definitions of burnout by generalizing that burnout is a negative internal psychological experience involving feelings, attitudes, motives, and expectations. Burnout can be considered one type of job stress. Although it has some of the same deleterious effects as other stress responses, burnout is unique in that the stress arises from the social interaction between the helper and recipient. At the heart of the burnout syndrome is a pattern of emotional overload and subsequent emotional exhaustion. For example, a life coach might become emotionally overinvolved with client concerns or challenges, overextend themselves, and then feel overwhelmed by the client's demands. The coach feels drained and used up, lacking the energy to face another day. Emotional resources are depleted and there is no source of replenishment in sight. The following quote helps us understand the experience of emotional exhaustion.

Coach #3

Everyday I was knocking myself out in my coaching practice—for the clients particularly, but also to prove to others (and myself) that I was a good coach. Before the day was even over, I was exhausted and emotionally drained. I just wanted to sit on the couch and cry. I needed a rest but couldn't seem to get away from the endless demands for my time. I felt so alone.

This emotional exhaustion is a common condition associated with the burnout syndrome. Once the emotional exhaustion sets in, helpers often feel they are unable to give anymore of themselves.

This development of a detached, indifferent response and disregard for others' needs and feelings marks a second characteristic of the burnout syndrome—depersonalization. Maslach (1982) reports that when individuals become soured by the press of humanity, they wish, at times, that other people would "get out of [their lives] and just leave [them] alone."

In the life coaching environment, it is not uncommon for coaches to encourage clients to check in anytime and discuss what's going on. Additionally, they support clients with supplemental handouts, reading assignments, or e-mails. If coaches do not set effective boundaries and monitor their commitments carefully, burnout may ensue. For any helping professional who experiences burnout, the almost constant contact with clients becomes too much. Seriously impaired helping professionals may even begin to resent the clients from whom there appears no escape.

Coach #4

I began to get extremely frustrated when clients would call or e-mail me between appointments even though I'd told them it was okay when we started and I'd be sure to respond quickly. I found myself caring less and developing a negative attitude. I didn't even want to return voice mail messages from clients to whom, only months before, I'd given huge amounts of time and attention.

Feelings of negativity toward others can progress until it turns to being negative toward oneself. Caregivers often feel disgrace or guilt about the way they have treated or thought about others; they sense that they are becoming the uncaring, cold type of person no one, especially themselves, wants to be around. Here, the third factor of burnout appears—a feeling of reduced personal accomplishment. Helping professionals may begin to develop a sense of inadequacy about their ability to relate to clients and this may result in the belief that they are a "failure." With this decline in self-esteem, depression may follow. Some coaches will seek assistance or be fortunate enough to have caring colleagues who intervene and help them gain perspective and balance. Others may leave coaching and abandon the work that they thought they'd loved so much. Sadly, the problem may well be that they loved their work too much and lost sight and perspective on the critical and holistic balance so necessary for well-being.

Coach Wellness and Self-care

Wellness is not a one-shot effort, a here-and-now philosophy. It promises an enhanced life-style, beginning at any point when deliberate conscious choices toward wellness are made. Given the integrated nature of human functions, any positive changes in any one aspect of functioning will lead to enhanced functioning in all areas. (Myers, 1991, p. 185)

Today, bookstores are brimming with a myriad of self-help books, tapes, guides, and resources to support anyone seeking a well-being perspective. Physical health issues have received more attention in part because physical illness is often the consequence for neglecting health and wellness activities. Health clubs, personal trainers, weight-loss groups, and physical fitness fundraisers, such as walks and races, are becoming more popular across the nation. Increasingly, popular and professional literature emphasize the important roles that spirituality, mental health, social adjustment, and other wellness dimensions play in a healthy and balanced lifestyle. Considerations of well-being and self-care are prominent in society at large and require the attention of life coaches.

Life is full, the pace is fast, and it even seems to be accelerating. Does it have to be this way? For many, the desire to end this craziness is strong. It is no surprise that books on simplicity are so popular these days. It is critical for life coaches to remember that, just like our clients, we have choices about how we live our lives and how we spend our time. We can continue doing things the way we do them and hope it gets better, or we can make necessary changes now.

Knowing versus Doing

We recognize that most of you who read this book know about burnout. You also probably know how to set boundaries, eat right, exercise, and practice great self-care. Please remember: *There is a world of difference between knowing what to do and actually doing it!!!* This is one reason why people need life coaches!

Bill Phillips describes a phenomenon in his book, *Body for Life* (1999), with people who said they wanted to start wellness programs. Many of the clients he worked with had all the knowledge they needed to begin a practice of healthy eating and regular exercise. They *knew* what they needed to do and yet repeatedly did not take action or quickly sabotaged their efforts by doing things they *knew* were not in their best interests. He calls this phenomenon "crossing the abyss." What he believes happens, and we certainly concur, is that what these people are missing is the ability to *apply* the knowledge. The same thing may happen with life coaches who begin to burn out. Without the ability to apply what you know, it doesn't matter how much you know—you'll still be stranded at the edge of an infinite abyss.

So how do you, as a helping professional considering a transition to life coaching (or a practicing life coach), cross the abyss of knowing about burnout and self-care to actually implementing it in your practice development? Let's take a look at where you are now.

TRY IT!

Take out your journal and answer the following question: For you to be pleased with your level of self-care, list the five most important, specific accomplishments you want to make, and intend to take on, within the next four weeks.

Take a few minutes to think about this and then list the accomplishments:

1.

2.

3.

4.

5.

It is a good sign if you found it easy to identify five *specific* actions you know you want to take between today and four weeks from today for you to be pleased with your level of self-care. This indicates you are looking forward with future vision.

If you struggled a bit to come up with five specific things you want to accomplish but you came up with two or three you were *really* confident of, you're on track but there is room for improvement.

If you found it extremely difficult to come up with any answers to the question or if it caught you completely off guard, you are not alone. The truth is, many people have a difficult time answering this simple question because it is not something most people can focus on. But if you really want to change and implement effective self-care strategies quickly in your life, you must move forward. And in order to *move forward, you must look forward.*

This is one of the major principles of life coaching. People whose daily actions are governed primarily by future vision constantly grow. They create, shape and modify their vision of the future. They create action plans and multiple pathways to get them where they need to go. They monitor their progress and adjust the route if they need to change course. It is like sailing a boat across a lake. Keeping in mind where you want to go (your future), and considering the changes in your environment, you take action to adjust your sails. The key pieces here are the future vision and the action. They will help you cross the abyss.

So, you've identified the five most important, specific accomplishments you want to make and within the next four weeks for you to be pleased with your level of self-care. If you haven't, do so now.

Here are some self-care accomplishments that both coaches and clients have told us they'd like to make. Perhaps they will help you think of some that would help you accomplish the level of self-care you desire.

Eat better.
Exercise more.
Stop giving all my time away to others.
Stop working too many hours.
Start flossing my teeth.
Stop drinking too much caffeine.

To help you take action, we suggest you view what you are doing now with regard to your self-care as *habit.* We believe habits can be changed. We constantly modify our own and we support our clients in doing the same.

TRY IT!

Get Specific: Pick three of the accomplishments you wrote down in your journal and commit to starting to implement them tomorrow. These are actions you believe will make a profound change in your self-care in the next four weeks. Write down *specific* actions you will take toward your accomplishments. Be specific! The more specific you are about what you want to accomplish, the more likely you will be to reach your goal. *(continued on next page)*

Here are some examples of actions:

"Get a massage every two weeks" is more specific than "Get some bodywork."

"Eat three servings of vegetables daily" is much more specific than "Eat more vegetables."

"Limit my coaching appointments to my established schedule, *no exceptions*," is much more specific than "Manage my schedule."

Monitor Your Progress: Using a form to monitor your progress is very helpful with changing habits. Coaches often provide their clients with forms to document habit change. To increase your likelihood of success, place the form in a prominent spot where you'll be sure to it every day.

Get Feedback and Support: Most of us know from experience how easy it is to plan to implement a change but not follow through on it completely. Usually we are successful for a few days, then something happens, and we slip back into our old habits.

The life coach is a valuable support person for the client who wants to change a habit. Similarly, we encourage you to pick carefully several appropriate support resources, but remember you are the most effective source for your own support. Getting a coach yourself, if you don't already have one, would be an excellent strategy. Faithfully using the habit change form and rewarding your own success will contribute to your progress. You may find examples of forms in *Co-Active Coaching* (pp. 210–211) and *Falling Awake* (pp. 208–209).

Practice, Practice, Practice: Most of us with therapy backgrounds know that practice is an effective tool for implementing behavior change. Just like learning any new and unfamiliar skill, the self-care habits you want to implement may feel uncomfortable or even foreign at first. Even if you experience some discomfort, keep your eye toward the future and keep practicing until the habit becomes natural. If you forget, or make a mistake, let go of self-criticism and get right back to your daily tracking. Specific strategies you can start using today to help you reach your self-care goals are monitoring your progress with the habits change form, using appropriate feedback and support, and practicing without blame.

Self-care Strategies from Practicing Life Coaches

We asked the faculty of and graduates from the Institute of Life Coach Training to share some of their self-care recommendations. The amount of responses was overwhelming. We were delighted to read about the effective strategies they employed in both their personal and coaching lives. We've included some specific responses, which we felt could help you get a clearer picture of what we mean by self-care and the variety of ways individuals implement it in their lives. We've also grouped the frequently repeated suggestions together for your benefit.

Here are what some of our life coaches have to say about self-care for your coaching practice.

Strategies for Balance by Jan Boxer

One week on/one week off—Since I have both a private (career and life coaching) practice and a corporate practice where I manage larger retainer-type contracts, I organize my time by spending one week focusing on private clients, then the next on corporate clients. On average I see (or telephone) each coaching client twice per month.

I hold a "case management"–type meeting with the coaches that subcontract from me (on the corporate side) once per month. We meet faithfully, even if we don't think there is much of an agenda, because it creates the opportunity to learn from one another. This collegial time fills me up emotionally and intellectually, reduces my stress by systematically providing me with a check-in time, and allows me to feel ready to account to the organizational client as necessary. Because I am working with other experienced coaches, most of what needs to be communicated about coachee progress or the lack thereof can wait until that meeting. This allows me to exchange sporadic telephone and e-mail contact with the coaches for something richer.

I never conduct more than two appointments back-to-back (assuming each appointment lasts for one and a half to two hours).

I take brief notes at the end of each session (some notes during as well), capturing the highlights of the discussion and the agreements about homework. This is usually a five-minute investment of time. I seldom feel panicked because of a lack of recall.

My favorite—taking clients outside! My corporate clients especially love this. We take walks, sit in the park, or share lunch at a cafe, etc. This helps me to maintain my energy, but it also helps them. They relax more than they do in an office and I get to the deeper stuff faster. I have been accused of this being a "technique." Coaches often realize they have shared more intimately than they may have in a business setting.

I make it known that I typically return calls between 5:00 and 6:00 PM and can usually be reached in my office at that time. I request that when leaving messages or e-mail that the caller or writer leave several options for meeting times. Once I have established a relationship (meaning we've met once or twice for an hourly fee), I move to a retainer agreement and a standing appointment (for example, every other Wednesday at 10:00). This simplifies scheduling and eliminates tons of telephone "tag."

I further protect myself by being clear about contracting, pricing, payment structures, etc. I use a separate financial agreement and outline the development program in another document.

On vacation I do not check voice mail or do anything related to work (except read).

When I am overwhelmed with commitments or my workload, I take a "time out" on all meetings that aren't urgent. Sometimes I take a three-month hiatus—I stop going to association meetings, networking events, book clubs, and some volunteer activities for a period of time. I find I have never missed as much as I imagined I would and the respite allows me to regain my focus and realign my priorities. I let group leaders know of my intent to return at a later date and thus far not suffered any repercussions (such as losing a client or affecting the overall contract).

Love Yourself by Roz Van Meter

I have a female client from Taiwan who has succeeded brilliantly in a mostly male industry. We were talking about taking care of yourself, and I used the expression "love yourself." She said her family, indeed her culture, didn't teach children how to do that. "How do you love yourself?" she asked. I hesitated for a moment, gathering my thoughts. How, indeed, do I love myself? I realized that I, too, had had to learn it as an adult. I told her about the following actions that I practice for self-care.

1. When I look in the mirror first thing in the morning, instead of telling myself how bad I look, I say to my reflection, "Bless your heart, you're getting to bed early tonight!"
2. When I leave voice-mail messages for myself, I say, "Hey, babe, don't forget to call Charles first thing tomorrow. 'Bye, Me."
3. I think of myself kindly, as I would a good friend. I try to be accepting and supportive of my efforts and acknowledge my frailties without defensiveness.
4. When I realize I'm in a toxic situation or relationship, I get myself out of there. After many years of always being the advocate for others, I've learned to be the advocate for myself.

After a short silence, my client said, and I could actually hear her beaming, "Thank you, Roz. I just realized I really *do* take care of myself."

Afterward I thought of all the things I didn't say—comfortable shoes, hugs from loved ones, the deliciousness of saying "no, thanks" when that's the honest answer, lazy days off, shrugging off the small stuff. It's taken me a lifetime to learn, but I do take care of myself. Here are some specific coaching self-care tips:

1. I have become more and more selective about my clients. I honor that little warning signal inside that says, "This person is not a fit for me."
2. Although I do 40-minute coaching calls, I schedule them every hour so I'll have a little decompression time.
3. I crave variety in my work so, along with my coaching business, I also maintain a therapy practice, write articles and books, give seminars, consult with corporations, and mentor emerging coaches.
4. I always build in play time. Every single day. An hour of fun with my husband, reading an intriguing book in bed, watching a favorite old film on TV.
5. I never forget that this is my life, the only one I'm likely to get, and I want to enjoy every minute of it.

Learn Important Lessons by Andy Viedrah

When I feel like I'm getting burned-out, I focus on making things simple. I feel that stress is just a mindset or perspective.

I have personally gone through burnout two or three times from being a therapist and entrepreneur. The first time was a result of my father's death in 1984 when I had to run his business with his partner until he bought out my mother's interest. I learned some important lessons about life and death.

One of the most important lessons I learned was the power of perspective. This is a little like reframing a bad situation into a good one. I take it down one notch by looking under the frame.

My reality is different from other people because I see life through my eyes only. To me life is like a glass of water; perspective tells you if it is half-empty or half-full. More to the point, it helps you decide if it is really important either way.

My Self-Care Story by Judy Girard

Self-care is a topic that has become near and dear to me. I had become acquainted with the term "extreme self-care" from Cheryl Richardson's first book, *Take Time for Your Life*. I had been exposed to the concept periodically over the years, but it always seemed to me to be something one did when things in your life weren't going well, like taking a bubble bath to relax when life had become so stressful you couldn't stand it one minute longer. Cheryl introduced me to the idea that this was something you did all the time. I took it seriously and embarked on a new adventure. After spending some time clarifying my values and the things that motivated me, I made some startling decisions in my life and took action.

I realized that not only did I not like what I was doing professionally, it was killing me literally. The constant stress had subjected me to constant physical pain and illness. I was doing some self-care at that time, but it almost felt futile. The futility was that the work I was engaged in was counteracting everything I was doing to care for myself. So, almost immediately, I quit my day job. I had conceptualized that I could do several other things and still survive financially. Part of that decision was a deeply felt belief that amazing things would not happen until I made room in my life for them. As long as I paid attention to things that were not important, I was not paying attention to things that were important. "Where your heart is, there your treasure is too." There was no room in my life as it was full of conflict and strife—those were the clients I dealt with each and every day.

I then started to make choices about what I did want in my life. I realized that I had allowed a lot of negative influences to infiltrate my life and that the time I was spending in some areas of my life was not a reflection of what I valued. I signed off of several e-mail distribution lists immediately and cut my e-mail and Internet time drastically. I did sign up for a few new e-mail lists—mostly daily inspirational stuff to help keep me on track.

With the things I had identified as my truest and deepest values as my foundation, I started instituting (or in some cases, continued with) some regular extreme self-care practices. Here are just a few big and little ones:

1. Daily prayer or meditation
2. Modifications in diet—I eliminated caffeine and processed sugar
3. Having lunch at least once a week with a friend or colleague
4. Utilizing my virtual assistant to manage less urgent business matters
5. Simplifying wherever possible—such as celebrating Thanksgiving on a day that's convenient to *everybody's* schedule
6. Not sweating the small stuff and staying focused

This list may make me seem like a spoiled brat. It sounds self-indulgent—and it is. But as a result, I am happier, more peaceful, more easygoing, and more authentic.

Remember You Are Unique by Monte Swan

Each life coach is unique and should not try to shoehorn him- or herself into a stereotype-model-formula-box. Living someone else's story is the main cause of negative stress in our lives. When we work and live from our own hearts, our lives are genuine, whimsical, and creative. Some things to remember:

1. Overload is caused by imbalance. We were created to rest one day a week.
2. Diet, exercise, rest, and personal relationships need to be balanced delicately.

Summary of Self-Care Recommendations
Personal Self-care

GET A COACH

If you intend to be a successful life coach, you need a coach. This is the most common recommendation we've received over the years from practicing coaches, especially those who are most successful. Many people beginning a coaching practice have never worked on their own and have no idea how difficult it is to stay focused and on task. A coach who is experienced at running a coaching practice will be a role model. You can learn how to be a better coach through participation in the coaching relationship and also experience what it is like to be a client.

You can locate a coach through a coach-training program like the Institute for Life Coach Training (see the Resources). If finances are tight at first, other options include sharing coaching with a buddy or triad coaching where A coaches B, B coaches C, and C coaches A in equal amounts of coaching time. When starting, we recommend you spend time with a "seasoned" coach or, at least, hire a mentor coach to help you with building your practice.

TAKE TIME FOR DESIGNING YOUR LIFE

Successful life coaches know that having a great life, or at least working toward one, is a characteristic of an effective life coach. This doesn't imply everything is always perfect for you but it does mean that you are attentive to creating the life of your dreams. We recommend you give attention to your whole life and continually create and implement new life plans and visions.

DE-CLUTTER YOUR LIFE

If you intend to make coaching a part of your life, something else will likely need to go. Successful coaches both physically and psychologically de-clutter their lives. They remove the energy drainers that suck off productive time. The list of energy drainers we discussed earlier is a good place to start looking at areas of your life that might benefit from de-cluttering.

PRACTICE EXTREME SELF-CARE

Again, this was high on the list of our coaches' recommendations. Extreme self-care is treating yourself to what you once might have considered a luxury. This is out-of-the-normal, regular, high-quality self-care. Examples might include a month-long vacation every year to someplace you *really* want to go, a regular massage, weekly manicures, a long bath, or not working until 10:00 AM after going to the gym for a workout and sauna. Another recommendation is to develop positive daily rituals that you choose to do. This might be meditation, journal writing, or anything that allows you to connect with your spiritual being.

PRACTICE PHYSICAL WELL-BEING AND MANAGE STRESS

These two go hand in hand; both are forms of self-care but our coaches set them apart for special emphasis. Eating well and getting exercise will help you manage stress. You should also practice lifetime wellness behaviors. If you aren't currently doing these, "crossing the abyss" from knowing to doing will be a valuable lesson for you as well as providing you with an important experience to share with your clients.

GET SUPPORT

Our coaches suggest that you carefully explain what you do to friends and family so they can understand your job and how it differs from therapy (if that was your previous line of work). This is especially important if you will be working from a home office. In this case, speaking with colleagues who have home offices can be especially valuable in learning and avoiding some of the pitfalls of working at home.

STRENGTHEN YOUR BOUNDARIES

You'll need strong boundaries to maintain a successful coaching practice and avoid burnout. You'll need to make time for your coaching practice *and* your life. Learn to say no unless the answer is definitely yes. Control your appointments and use your day—don't let your day use you. Go back and clarify your coaching practice and self-care visions. If it isn't what you want and doesn't fit into your future plans . . . don't do it!

Business Self-care

Our life coaches had numerous suggestions about taking care of your business. We have listed some here.

MANAGE THE SIZE OF YOUR PRACTICE

When you build your business and determine how often you want to work, etc., *stick to it!* If you want to add workshops or teach a coaching class, either reduce your amount of clients or expand the time and energy you have available for appointments and business activities. Make choices about your coaching practice consciously and in light of your general life goals.

CREATE AN IDEAL CALENDAR

Mark off an ideal time for client appointments and stick to it! Schedule time for self-care and other activities that you want in your life. For example, if you really want to write and morning is a good time for you to think creatively, mark it off!

Some coaches find, as their practice grows, they work six straight hours with no breaks. One way to avoid this is to put your breaks on the schedule before you schedule your appointments. We highly recommend this practice.

Also, block your clients together on days and times that you want to work, not when they find it most convenient. Having client appointments scattered all over your calendar is frustrating. You will be more energized for your calls and provide more quality time in your schedule for other things you want in your life if you make appointments in blocks of time.

TAKE TIME OFF

Many of our coaches recommend scheduled breaks from your coaching practice. This includes breaks in your coaching day but also days off when you do not work on your coaching business. Self-employed individuals are notorious for not taking time off. Don't fall prey to this trap. Additionally, we highly recommend taking vacations—not working vacations—to get away from it all and do something fun. Plan ahead and put it in your schedule! Many coaches schedule appointments only three times a month, which frees up several weeks a year to do office work, marketing, or better yet, take time off.

ALLOW TIME "AROUND" YOUR APPOINTMENTS

Several experienced coaches strongly recommend allowing time for pre-session focus and post-session reflection between appointments. This provides you a scheduled time to review your client notes from a previous session before the next call or session so you are prepared. Reflection afterwards allows thoughtful attention about how the session went and future actions you might take. Jumping from one session immediately into another is a sure recipe for burnout over the long haul.

REFER EXCESS CLIENTS TO OTHER COACHES

Keep a list of coaches whom you trust that will take referrals. After the initial stages of practice building, our coaches strongly recommend that you develop an active habit of referring clients who don't meet your ideal client profile. Most coach training programs or mentor coaches will help you identify your ideal client. Avoid the trap of taking just anybody, especially when your intuition tells you the client isn't a "fit." Instead, give that person an effective referral to another coach. Likewise, even when you really want to work with a client, refer him or her if you are booked. Unless you will have an opening in the near future, it is fairer for all your clients, as well possible new ones, if you make a referral rather than overloading your practice to the detriment of all . . . including you!

Like everyone else, life coaches need to grow personally and professionally. You've read about some of the activities our coaches practice to care for themselves and some of their recommendations for keeping their practices vibrant. We recommend your professional growth include membership and participation in the International Coach Federation (ICF). The ICF is a great support source for new and established coaches, and their annual conference is a wonderful opportunity to take advantage of continuing education opportunities and to network with colleagues.

Before moving on to chapter 13 to examine the future of life coaching, take time to reflect on your learning about self-care. Complete the Try it! exercise, which will help you determine what you want in your life coaching practice and focus your attention on personal action steps that will help you cross the abyss from knowing to doing.

TRY IT!

1. What are four strategies for having a balanced practice that you want to employ in your life coaching practice? You may use your journal or write them in the spaces below.

(continued on next page)

2. What action steps do you intend to take in the next ten days to help you implement those strategies?

3. How will you monitor your progress?

4. Who will you use for support and feedback?

There are many wonderful aspects to the life coaching profession. However, as you've read, the stresses do not disappear just because you leave the traditional therapeutic model. You will need to change how you are *with* the world and *in* the world if you truly want to take on an active practice of extreme self-care. We make self-care a daily habit, and our lives are richer and our practices are more rewarding because of this important decision.

CHAPTER THIRTEEN

The Future of Coaching

The future belongs to those who believe in the beauty of their dreams.

—Eleanor Roosevelt

Is coaching a passing fancy or is it the true evolution of a new profession? Several indicators point to coaching being a new profession that is establishing itself within the framework of existing helping professions. First, the establishment of a professional organization—the International Coach Federation—and associated ethical standards and minimal competencies, predict the continuation of this profession. Second, the number of practicing coaches (which the ICF estimates at 10,000) is growing rapidly and responding clearly to the needs and demands of our fast-paced, disconnected society. Third, there is evidence of an increasing number of recognized coach-training organizations and a growing number of college courses on coaching, which further establishes the profession within the mainstream of continuing education for professionals.

Perhaps coaching would be just a passing fad if not for its widespread appeal to the general population, which provides a powerful motivation for continued growth and success for individuals and organizations. The growth of the life coaching profession specifically, as we indicated earlier, had many of its roots in the corporate world of mentoring and executive coaching. However, in the early 1990s, personal coaching burst upon the scene with the creative vision of Thomas Leonard (founder of Coach University) and some of the other coach-training schools (see the Resources section). The coaching movement has been fueled by the concept and attractiveness of personal coaching. It is a very palatable concept for the self-employed entre-preneur, or corporate refugee who wants to design a life and career that blends with their larger life's purpose. Coaching continues to grow and evolve in the corporate setting and is a powerful technology for retaining employees, developing leaders, and even transforming the corporate culture of a company. However, we believe that if coaching had only been seen as a corporate phenomenon, it would have rapidly disappeared just like Total Quality Management (TQM), Quality circles, T-groups, Theory X, Theory Y, and other associated "quick fix" strategies. Instead, the quality of a well-trained, personally hired coach, coupled with the internal coaches in corporations, makes it increasingly likely this popular profession will continue to grow in scope and recognition.

Another powerful attraction of life coaching is that having a personal life coach provides a partner who really cares about helping you develop and implement your ideal life. Life coaching also gives a sense of connection, of belonging, of significance in a world that can sometimes seem isolating, overwhelming, or both. Coaches also keep us focused, challenged, and moti-vated for living our lives (personally and professionally) *on purpose*. We both have our own coaches for those very reasons.

It is our hope that life coaching, in all its various forms, will begin to per-meate society at all levels. We want to see coaches in schools, probation departments, churches, nonprofit corporations, and other community agen-cies. In reality, this has already begun to happen. Coaching is a combination of communication and empowerment that should become ingrained into our entire cultural fabric so that relationships at all levels can implement the coaching paradigm as a new and effective way to bring out the best in people and create solutions to complex problems.

We do believe psychotherapy has played an important role in those who are lives of many clients and that psychotherapy will still be needed in our society, especially for those who are seriously mentally ill. However, it has also pathologized a significant number of individuals with sometimes meaningless and unnecessary labels. We believe coaching will become the prevailing way to get help or to learn how to bring out your strengths and overcome obsta-cles and challenges while pursuing possibilities. We believe this is what the human potential movement of the 1970s intended. Psychological research and theory of the last several decades have contributed much to our understand-ing of how people change, how they adjust to life's struggles, and how they develop into self-actualized human beings. That knowledge now lends itself to this new field of life coaching, without the stigma and labeling that comes with psychological counseling or therapy. Being able to receive coaching and have a personal coach, whether privately hired or provided by your company or community agency, is a service we hope becomes ubiquitous and transformational to individuals and our culture as a whole.

Another important factor in any new profession to be accepted widely is publicity and public awareness. The media over the last several years have overwhelmingly said positive things about coaching. There have been many articles about coaching, its impact and value to clients, and the level of professionalism in the field. In fact, after Pat was interviewed for a magazine article on two different occasions, the reporters asked to set up coaching appointments for themselves. Even though anybody can call him- or herself a coach, the quality of people with this title is very high. Many have come from other professions such as law, ministry, or psychology; others are corporate refugees, human resource professionals, or experienced consultants.

Although there are many coach-training programs and certification is available through the ICF and other programs, certification is not necessary. However, professional training and strong ethics are important. After all, consultants have never been certified nor licensed; they only get continued work through their reputations and previous work histories.

We can assume that, as the profession grows, coaching will attract its share of charlatans or unscrupulous business people. But these coaches without ethics and experience will not last long and will fade away quickly. The marketplace for coaches is expanding to the point where anyone who is currently a consultant, trainer, minister, manager, or helping professional is either now learning specific coaching skills or expanding the scope of what they offer to include coaching. Coaching has become an umbrella under which many forms of personal services fit.

Emerging Trends in Coaching

Looking into our crystal ball, we do see some emerging trends that may be on the cutting edge of coaching or may become innovative ways for the public to access the benefits of coaching.

1. **Coach on call.** Sometimes called "spot coaching" or "just-in-time coaching," this is brief coaching available to the client at the moment they need it. A client might have a coach or coaching service on retainer by paying

a monthly fee but can call whenever they need support, direction, or motivation. Pat is part of a group of coaches called The Coaching Collective, which provides people with brief conversations by appointment or during set office hours from any one of 12 coaches; clients pay a flat fee of $95 per month to belong to the group. Clients may also participate in classes, book discussions, or a group coaching experience called Collective Wisdom where four or five coaches, led by a conductor, offer coaching to one client at a time for 10 to 15 minutes. As reported by the clients, these brief coaching experiences, often lead to breakthroughs. This process is innovative, powerful, and fun.

2. **Videoconference coaching.** Some coaches now coach via e-mail but usually as an added service, not as the primary vehicle for coaching. With the increasing availability of video communication by personal computer, however, this will increase as a way to connect with clients. There is even technology available that provides virtual classrooms and chat rooms, allowing the instructor or coach the ability to separate participants with different assignments or conversations. Though this technology is still expensive, it will become more mainstream in the years to come. The ease of real-time visual communication with technologies on the horizon are going to make global coaching an increasingly available opportunity.

3. **Agency coaches.** We both really see the strong probability of agencies, churches, schools, probation departments, etc., adding staff positions for coaches. What happens in business usually is mirrored in nonprofit agencies and public service agencies.

What the Future Holds

We are on the verge of a fundamental shift in how and why people seek helpers. People today need connection with a mentor, coach, or guide more than ever before, due to the rapid pace of change, the difficulty of sustainable relationships, or the desire to fulfill one's life purpose.

We believe that the profession of coaching soon will be bigger than psychotherapy. The general public will know the distinction between therapy and coaching and will be clear on when to seek a therapist and when to seek a coach. Coaching will permeate society and be available to everyone—not just executives or high-powered professionals. We expect to see a variety of specialized coaches like relationship coaches, parenting and family coaches, wellness and health coaches, spiritual development coaches, and others.

The entire profession, as we see it, will foster the idea of life coaching as the umbrella under which all coaching rests. Whether a client seeks specific coaching for business or job challenges, coaching for a life transition (such as a career change, relationship loss, or health), or for pure life-design coaching, it is all life coaching. A coach may also serve as a referral source for specialty coaching as needed or requested by their client.

Coaching is a profession that is experiencing dynamic growth and change. It will no doubt continue to interact developmentally with social, economic, and political processes; draw on the knowledge base of diverse disciplines; enhance its intellectual and professional maturity; and proceed to establish itself internationally and in mainstream America. If these actions represent the future of coaching, then the profession will change in ways that support viability and growth. Life coaching exists because it is helpful, and it will prosper because it can be transformational.

Common Questions from Aspiring Life Coaches

Q: Can I transition a therapy client into a coaching client? How?

A: Current or former clients who see you as a therapist may become qualified coaching clients if they do not have a *DSM-IV* diagnosis that needs treatment and if they understand that coaching with you is *not* therapy. We recommend that you have some ritual ending within the therapy relationship, then start anew with a coaching intake packet and meet in a different location or over the telephone. The coaching relationship and coaching services must be seen as separate and unique from psychotherapy. A rule we both live by and urge therapists to follow is that if a former therapy client decides to hire you as a coach, you should be clear that you can never again be his or her therapist. It is too important to keep the professions separate and you cannot be both someone's therapist and coach. You can use coaching skills with a therapy client, but that is not the same as having a professional coaching relationship with him or her.

Q: What if I start out coaching someone and it becomes clear that he or she also needs therapy?

A: This is actually a good service of coaching. Many clients can still have a coach and engage a therapist concurrently. We suggest you keep very clear boundaries from what is covered in therapy and what happens in coaching. For example, we have coached clients who we referred to couples therapy, grief work, divorce counseling, etc. but also continued to be their life coach. What is important here is that you do not try to be both a therapist and coach. It is too confusing and unethical to shift between professional roles.

As a trained professional therapist, when, as a coach, you feel it is appropriate to refer your coaching client to a therapist, you might have a conversation with the client about recommended therapists or at least types of therapy that could be most beneficial. Coach your client on questions to ask, what to look for, and whatever else can open the door for your client's finding the most appropriate psychotherapist.

Q: Let's say someone comes in for a therapy consultation and I think she could benefit from life coaching instead. How do I handle that?

A: That is one way a therapist might get some initial coaching clients. Many people seek help with life transitions or a lack of direction in their lives and that is how they get to a therapist. When life coaching is explained to them and they see that the coach is their partner in designing the life they want to live, they often get excited about the coaching relationship. Again, however, you must be very clear that if they hire you as their life coach, you are not providing psychotherapy or acting as a therapist.

Q: How do I handle it when someone has hired me as his coach, and, within a few sessions, I discover that he really needs psychological help?

A: Again, that is the value of you being the client's coach. Have a coaching conversation about what you are experiencing and think about his potential need for professional psychotherapy. Discuss your thoughts and reasons and see if he agrees. Then, provide some referrals if you can or at least direct him to the type of therapy you would recommend. You can continue to coach him if the psychological help can be separate. If he needs therapy before he is coachable and is able to make strides toward a desired future, then coaching can be put on hold.

Q: What are the issues of liability in coaching? Should I carry liability insurance?

A: Liability in coaching has proven to be extremely minimal, especially if you are clear about not giving advice or professional recommendations. As a coach you are working with clients mutually to decide the steps they want to take, objectives they want to commit to, and changes they want to make in their lives. Coaching clients should not be emotionally fragile persons and are assumed to be capable of making clear personal choices in their life.

Liability insurance is available for coaching professionals through the International Coach Federation (www.coachfederation.org) and through private business insurers. In some cases, therapists have included coaching in their current professional liability insurance. You must check with your insurer for information on this topic.

Q: How do I know if I am doing a good job as a coach?

A: We have two answers: Ask your client and work with your own coach on this. Really, it is very powerful to ask your client periodically, "Is the coaching valuable to you?" or "I really want our coaching to be extremely valuable and effective for you . . . is there any way I could coach you better?"

Q: What are the essential details to cover in the first interview or coaching session?

A: This is really covered in detail in a coach-training program but, in a nut-shell, we recommend that you have already sent the client your welcome packet, which includes forms for listing desired goals, current energy drainers, things that are frustrating or in the way of the life he or she wants, etc. Then in the first session, you review these forms and discuss some short-term and immediate action steps that will lead to fulfilling any short-term goals that fit with the client's long-term vision and life purpose.

Q: What do I do if I have a resistant client?

A: Resistance is a term we are very familiar with as therapists. Get it out of your vocabulary in coaching. If you have clients who seem unable to take the desired action steps or keep coming to sessions with no successful follow-through, the next coaching conversation should be about your observation. In other words, as their coach, you are not looking for underlying reasons or neuroses for their "resistance" but instead coaching them toward possibilities and action. If they seem stuck, ask them how the coaching can be changed to have them get what they want. If that does not work, then suggest that coaching seems not to be right for them at that point and to reconsider it when they are ready to make big changes in their life. We call that a courageous conversation and using compassionate edge as a coach.

Q: What do I do if I sense tension in my coaching relationship or if I come to dislike my client?

A: It is part of the honesty and authenticity of the coach to have a conversation about this. As the coach you model effective communication by not stepping over or around conflict or tension in the relationship. You can actually use this honest conversation as powerful coaching. Frame it as your perception only and ask the client how she sees or experiences it and then make the necessary changes if you can.

Q: Do you have to like your clients to be an effective coach for them?

A: We really believe that you do. As therapists, this was not necessary, but in coaching, at least for us, we want to work with people whom we like or at least don't have any negative feelings toward. You will like some clients better than others, but we do believe that it is part of the coaching relationship to coach people you really want to work with and whom you really enjoy coaching.

Q: How does termination with a coaching client compare with termination with a therapy client?

A: The word termination sounds so clinical. In coaching, you do want to formalize when the coaching relationship is complete or ending temporarily. But you do not have to be as clinical or detailed as you would be in therapy. You should mutually decide (prompted by the coaching client) that you are ending or stopping the formal coaching relationship, but make it clear that the door is always open. Your client will really give clues as to when coaching is no longer needed or desired. You have the task of frequently checking on the client's perceived value, but it is the client who usually determines whether it is time to stop. We do believe that you should consider a final review session that summarizes the coaching progress and then end the session with what the next steps are for the client. Then let him know that he can always work with you again or you can refer him to another coach when he desires.

Q: Do coaches use some of the techniques from solution-focused therapy such as scaling questions, the miracle question, or pattern interruption?

A: Absolutely! Anything you have used as a therapist that can forward a client into action is equally powerful in coaching. Use whatever works from solution-focused techniques, Ericksonian strategies, NLP, cognitive therapy techniques, reality therapy, choice theory, and so on.

Q: Do you find that your therapist license is helpful or distracting for clients to be aware of?

A: We always recommend you keep your therapy practice and your coaching business separate. It is great that you have a graduate degree and that does add to credibility. But coaching clients do not need to know that you are a licensed therapist. If they do, be clear that you are their coach and not their therapist. This separation is also important to maintain to decrease liability.

Q: If you offer primarily telephone coaching, how do you make up for the lack of visual cues?

A. This is one of the real surprises of telephone coaching. We and other coaches have noticed that since we are working with functionally healthy individuals as our coaching clients, we do not need to be as tuned into visual clues. In fact, the telephone relationship has fewer distractions and can be more focused than a face-to-face session. You seem to be able to create the necessary intimacy and sacred space in the telephone relationship and use the time efficiently and powerfully. We ask our clients to send us pictures of themselves and they can see pictures of us on our Web site. These visual aids add to the personal quality in the coaching relationship and provide a visual framework.

Q: How "self-actualized" do you have to be as a life coach to be successful?

A: Obviously, you are in the position of being a model for your clients. But that does not mean you have to be a guru or realized master to be a coach! You do, however, need to be aware of the areas in your life that are evolving and you cannot be an effective coach if your life is in more disarray than your clients' lives. The keys are awareness and action. If you are working on goals similar to your client (such as more effective time management, better organization, improved life habits, etc.), then you can model the path while you are also on it.

Q: Do you have to live in a major metropolitan area to be a successful personal coach?

A: In many ways it is easier to make important business connections in a large city, but we know several coaches in very remote rural settings who have full practices. Using your computer and telephone, you can develop a virtual community of contacts across the globe. Marketing a coaching business in a rural locale takes some creative planning and nontraditional ways to get the word out, but in today's high-tech world, it is easier than you think.

Q: Can personal coaching be done on-line via e-mail communication?

A: Yes, however neither of us promote that as the best form of coaching. We feel that telecoaching still has a strong personal connection and find that cybercoaching via e-mail exclusively misses that personal touch. However, there are coaches who do on-line coaching and use chat lines and other real-time formats. E-mail coaching is a great adjunct to regular telephone calls and a valuable added service to a coaching relationship.

Q: What about the professional ethics and standards of confidentiality we as therapists are used to?

A: That is one reason we believe that therapists make such great coaches. They come from a profession that highly values ethics and professional standards. There are guidelines on the ethics of coaching created by the International Coaching Federation (see p. 184) and, as a coach, you should always be as ethical as you were as a therapist. You always respect the confidentiality of your clients, but interestingly you will find that coaching clients are less formalized with their need to have the coaching relationship be confidential. They are often happy to tell people you are their coach and you can also have a more friendly relationship with coaching clients than with therapy clients.

Resources

Assessments

Information on the DISC and PIAV: www.ttidisc.com.

Information on the PeopleMap: www.peoplemap-training.com.

Information on the Firo-B: www.discoveryourpersonality.com

Information on 360-degree assessment: assessmentspecialists.com/cp.html.

Information on Myers-Briggs: www.knowyourtype.com.

Information on 16PF: www.hr2000.com.

Associations

Association of Humanistic Psychology. 45 Franklin St., #315, San Francisco, CA 94102. Phone: 415-864-8850. Fax: 864-8853. E-mail: AHPOffice@aol.com. Web site: www.ahpweb.org.

International Coach Federation. 1444 I Street NW, Suite 700, Washington, DC 20005. Phone: 888-3131 or 202-712-9039. Fax: 888-329-2423 or 202-216-9646. E-mail: icfoffice@coachfederation.org. Web site: www.coachfedera-tion.org.

Bridge Lines

Available by the hour: Institute for Life Coach Training: info@lifecoachtraining.com or 888-267-1206.

Available by the month: Sparck International: 702-252-0070; Webvalence. com: 503-335-3442; EntertainmentU: 212-333-7400; Teleclass International: 877-550-9282.

Coaching Books

Cameron, J. (1992). *The artist's way: A spiritual path to higher creativity.* Los Angeles, CA: Tarcher/Perigee.

Ellis, D. (2000). *Falling awake: Creating the life of your dreams.* Rapid City, SD: Breakthrough Enterprises.

Fortgang, L. B. (1998). *Take yourself to the top: The secrets of America's #1 career coach.* New York, NY: Warner.

Fortgang, L. B. (2001). *Living your best life: Ten strategies for getting from where you are to where you're meant to be.* New York: Tarcher/Putnam.

Hargrove, R. A. (1995). *Masterful coaching: Extraordinary results by impacting people and the way they think and work together.* San Diego: Pfeiffer & Co.

Hudson, F. M. (1999). *The handbook of coaching: A comprehensive resource guide for managers, executives, consultants, and human resource professionals.* San Francisco: Jossey-Bass.

Leonard, T. J. (1998). *The portable coach: 28 surefire strategies for business and personal success.* New York: Scribner.

McGraw, P. C. (1999). *Life strategies: Doing what works, doing what matters.* New York: Hyperion.

McGraw, P. C. (2000). *The life strategies workbook: Exercises and self-tests to help you change your life.* New York: Hyperion.

McGraw, P. C. (2000). *Relationship rescue: A seven step strategy for reconnecting with your partner.* New York: Hyperion.

Richardson, C. (1998). *Take time for your life: A personal coach's seven-step program for creating the life you want.* New York: Broadway.

Richardson, C. (2000). *Life makeovers: 52 practical and inspiring ways to improve your life one week at a time.* New York: Broadway.

Robinson, L. A. (2001). *Divine intuition.* New York: DK.

Whitmore, J. (1996). *Coaching for performance.* Sonoma, CA: N. Brealey.

Coach Training

Institute for Life Coach Training. Patrick Williams, President. 2801 Wakonda Drive, Ft. Collins, CO 80521. Phone: 1-888-267-1206. Fax: 970-224-9832. E-mail: info@lifecoachtraining.com. Web site: www.lifecoachtraining. com. The Institute also offers both tele-classes and live classes for therapists transitioning to coaching.

You may also seek other coach training opportunities at www.coachfederation.org.

Home Business

Baker, S., & Baker, K. (1988). *The ultimate home office survival guide.* Princeton, NJ: Peterson's.

Bond, W. J. (1997). *Going solo: Developing a home-based consulting business from the ground up.* New York: McGraw-Hill.

Edwards, P., & Edwards, S. (1996). *Finding your perfect work: The new career guide to making a living, creating a life.* New York: Putnam.

Edwards, P., & Edwards, S. (1999). *Working from home: everything you need to know about living and working under the same roof.* New York: Tarcher/Putnam.

Edwards, P., Edwards, S., & Economy, P. (2000). *Home-based business for dummies.* Indianapolis: IDG.

Gilkerson, L. D., & Paauwe, T. M. (1998). *Self-employment: From dream to reality!* Indianapolis: JIST Works.

Godin, S. (1998). *If you're clueless about starting your own business and want to know more.* Chicago: Upstart.

Grodzki, L. (2000). *Building your ideal private practice.* New York: Norton.

Lesonsky, R. (2001). *Start your own business: The only start-up book you'll ever need.* Irvine, CA: Entrepreneur.

Lonier, T. (1994). *Working solo: The real guide to freedom and financial success with your own business.* New York: Wiley.

Peterson, C. D. (1997). *On your own: Discovering your new life and career beyond the corporation.* New York: Wiley.

Zelinsky, M. (1999). *Practical home office solutions.* New York: McGraw-Hill.

INTERNATIONAL COACH FEDERATION

The ICF Philosophy and Definition of Coaching

The International Coach Federation adheres to a form of coaching that honors the client as the expert in his/her personal and/or professional life and believes that every client is creative, resourceful, and whole. Standing on this foundation, the coach's responsibility is to:

1. Discover, clarify, and align with what the client wants to achieve
2. Encourage client self-discovery
3. Elicit client-generated solutions and strategies
4. Hold the client as responsible and accountable

Definition of Coaching

Professional Coaching is an ongoing partnership that helps clients produce fulfilling results in their personal and professional lives. Through the process of coaching, clients deepen their learning, improve their performance, and enhance their quality of life.

In each meeting, the client chooses the focus of conversation, while the coach listens and contributes observations and questions. This interaction creates clarity and moves the client into action. Coaching accelerates the client's progress by providing greater focus and awareness of choice. Coaching concentrates on where clients are today and what they are willing to do to get where they want to be tomorrow.

Pledge of Ethics

As a professional coach, I acknowledge and honor my ethical obligations to my coaching clients and colleagues and to the public at large. I pledge to comply with ICF Standards of Ethical Conduct, to treat people with dignity as free and equal human beings, and to model these standards with those whom I coach. If I breach this Pledge of Ethics or any ICF Standards of Ethical Conduct, I agree that the ICF in its sole discretion may hold me accountable for so doing. I further agree that ICF's holding me accountable for my breach may include loss of my ICF membership or my ICF certification.

ICF Standards of Ethical Conduct

- I will conduct myself in a manner that reflects well on coaching as a profession and I will refrain from doing anything that harms the public's understanding or acceptance of coaching as a profession.
- I will identify my level of coaching competence to the best of my ability and I will not overstate my qualifications, expertise or experience as a coach.
- I will, at the beginning of each coaching relationship, ensure that my coaching client understands the terms of the coaching agreement between us.
- I will not claim or imply outcomes that I cannot guarantee.
- I will respect the confidentiality of my client's information, except as otherwise authorized by my client or as required by law.
- I will obtain permission from each of my clients before releasing their names as clients or references.
- I will be alert to noticing when my client is no longer benefiting from our coaching relationship and thus would be better served by another coach or by another resource and, at that time, I will encourage my client to make that change.
- I will avoid conflicts between my interests and the interests of my clients.
- Whenever the potential for a conflict of interest arises, I will, on a timely basis, discuss the conflict with my client to reach informed agreement with my client on how to deal with it in whatever way best serves my client.
- I will, on a timely basis, disclose to my client all compensation from third parties that I may receive for referrals of, or advice given to, that client.
- I will honor every term of agreements I make with my clients and, if separate, with whoever compensates me for the coaching of my clients.
- I will not give my clients or any prospective clients information or advice I know to be confidential, misleading or beyond my competence.
- I will acknowledge the work and contributions of others; I will respect copyrights, trademarks, and intellectual property rights, and I will comply with applicable laws and my agreements concerning these rights.

The Welcome Packet

The following pages contain examples of typical forms in a welcome packet. You may adapt any of these to suit your needs.

Your Name and Contact Information Goes Here

CLIENT POLICIES AND PROCEDURES

Welcome!

Welcome to coaching as my client. I look forward to working together. There are a few guidelines that I expect clients to maintain in order for our relationship to work. If you have any questions, please call me.

Fee	Clients pay me on time unless prior arrangements have been made. Payment may be made by check or credit card.
Procedure	My clients call on time. Come to the call with updates, progress and current challenges. Let me know what you want to work on, and be ready to be coached. **Make copies of the enclosed client prep form and fax or e-mail a completed form before each call. The agenda is client generated and coach supported.**
Calls	Our agreement includes a set amount of calls. If you or I are on vacation, we spend more time before you/I leave and after you/I return.
Changes	My clients give me 24 hours notice if they have to cancel or reschedule a call. If you have an emergency, we will work around it. Otherwise, a missed call is not made up.
Extra Time	You may call between sessions if you need "spot coaching", have a problem, or can't wait to share a win with me. (You can also fax or e-mail me). I enjoy delivering this extra level of service. I do not bill for additional time of this type, but I ask that you please keep the extra calls to five or ten minutes. When you leave a message, let me know if you want a call back or if you are just sharing.
Problems	I want you to be satisfied with our relationship. If I ever say or do something that upsets you or doesn't feel right, please bring it up. I promise to do what is necessary to have you be satisfied.
A Must	It is necessary for the client to implement the coaching that is given to feel that coaching is a success. You have hired a coach to do things differently than you ever have before. If you choose to not use the coaching and keep doing what you have always done, you will get the results you have always gotten.

LIFE COACHING AGREEMENT

To my client: Please review, adjust, sign where indicated, and return to me at the above address.

Name_____

Initial term _____ Months, from_____ through_____

Fee $ _____ Per month, $_____ For the project

Session date _____ Session time _____

Number of sessions per month_____

Duration _____(length of scheduled session)

Referred by_____

Ground rules: 1. Client calls the coach at the scheduled time.
2. Client pays coaching fees in advance.
3. Client pays for long-distance charges, if any.

1. As a client, I understand and agree that I am fully responsible for my well-being during my coaching calls, including my choices and decisions. I am aware that I can choose to discontinue coaching at any time. I recognize that coaching is not psychotherapy and that professional referrals will be given if needed.

2. I understand that "life coaching" is a relationship I have with my coach that is designed to facilitate the creation/development of personal, professional or business goals and to develop and carry out a strategy/plan for achieving those goals.

3. I understand that life coaching is a comprehensive process that may involve all areas of my life, including work, finances, health, relationships, education and recreation. I acknowledge that deciding how to handle these issues and implement my choices is exclusively my responsibility.

4. I understand that life coaching does not treat mental disorders as defined by the American Psychiatric Association. I understand that life coaching is not a substitute for counseling, psychotherapy, psychoanalysis, mental health care or substance abuse treatment and I will not use it in place of any form of therapy.

5. I promise that if I am currently in therapy or otherwise under the care of a mental health professional, that I have consulted with this person regarding the advisability of working with a life coach and that this person is aware of my decision to proceed with the life coaching relationship.

6. I understand that information will be held as confidential unless I state otherwise, in writing, except as required by law.

7. I understand that certain topics may be anonymously shared with other life-coaching professionals for training OR consultation purposes.

8. I understand that life coaching is not to be used in lieu of professional advice. I will seek professional guidance for legal, medical, financial, business, spiritual or other matters. I understand that all decisions in these areas are exclusively mine and I acknowledge that my decisions and my actions regarding them are my responsibility.

I have read and agree to the above.

Client signature_____

Date _____

CLIENT DATA FORM

Date: _____

Name: _____

Occupation: _____

Business name: _____

Home address: _____ ☐ Preferred address

_____

_____

Business address: _____ ☐ Preferred address

_____

Day phone: _____ Evening phone: _____

Fax line: _____ Cell phone: _____

E-mail address: _____

Okay to leave messages everywhere? _____ If not, explain: _____

_____

Preferred means of communication: _____

Date of birth: _____ Age: _____

Other significant dates: _____

Preferred coaching schedule:

on (day of week) _____ or (time of day) _____

Names of important people in your life (spouse, partner, children, friends, etc.): _____

_____

_____

Emergency contact: _____

Other information you want me to know: (You may continue on back of page.) _____

_____

_____

How did you hear about my coaching services? _____

What influenced your decision to work with a coach?

_____

_____

_____

Have you ever been coached? If so, please describe the experience.

_____

_____

_____

Do you have specific goals for the coaching relationship? If not, what goals might you now create?

_____

_____

_____

_____

_____

_____

_____

What are your significant commitments?

_____

_____

_____

_____

What would your perfect life look like?

_____

_____

_____

_____

What are your dreams?

_____

_____

_____

What dreams have you given up on?

_____

_____

_____

Where do you want to focus first?

_____

_____

_____

_____

What parts of your life are working best now?

_____

_____

_____

_____

What parts of life are working least well?

_____

_____

_____

_____

What are your values?

_____

_____

_____

_____

What stops you from having the life you want to have?

_____

_____

_____

_____

YOUR LIFE STORY

(Please write in any style you desire and be as creative as you want. Detail any important aspects, accomplishments, highlights that you feel are important for me to know. **Please send this with a recent picture if we are coaching by phone.**)

_____

_____

_____

_____

_____

_____

_____

_____

_____

_____

_____

_____

_____

_____

_____

_____

_____

_____

_____

_____

_____

_____

_____

_____

_____

_____

THE FIRST STEP: DE-CLUTTERING

We put up with, accept, take on, and are dragged down by people and situations that we may have come to ignore in our lives rather than fix them. Now is the time to identify those things that drain your energy for positive activities. As you think of more items, add them to your list.

You may or may not choose to do anything about them right now, but just becoming aware of and articulating them will bring them to the forefront where you'll naturally start eliminating, fixing, or resolving them.

ENERGY DRAINERS AT WORK	ENERGY DRAINERS AT HOME
1)	1)
2)	2)
3)	3)
4)	4)
5)	5)
6)	6)
7)	7)
8)	8)
9)	9)
10)	10)
11)	11)
12)	12)
13)	13)
14)	14)
15)	15)
16)	16)
17)	17)
18)	18)
19)	19)
20)	20)

LIFE BALANCE WHEEL
(Coaching Mandala)

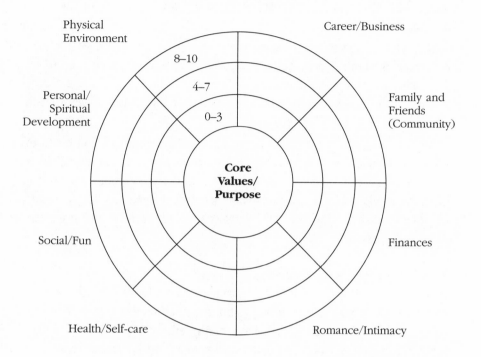

© Dr. Patrick Williams
Institute for Life Coach Training

The hub represents your core values—each area interrelated in an ideal life. Give yourself a score (1–10) and shade or color in the space accordingly. Use this Coaching Mandala as a way to assess the level of life satisfaction in each area. You may score it numerically to measure the improvement desired, or you may use it to have a coaching conversation about gaps between where you are now and where you would like to be.

TEMPLATE FOR PERSONAL VISION STATEMENT

I strongly believe that we are each the creator and director of our own life drama, able to create "on purpose" what our life will look like, feel like, and be like.

It is your opportunity and responsibility to write the script, be the producer and director, and to gather the other characters in your life drama. Some people live painful dramas or unfulfilling dramas, but if you are conscious and on purpose with what you want your life to be, it has a much greater chance of evolving into your vision.

So how does one begin designing one's life? First of all you can begin to revisit and remember dreams and desires from your younger years. What drove you? What did you want to become? Who did you admire? Divide your life into thirds and ask yourself what accomplishments or happy events occurred in each third of your life? What values were represented? Are those values still present?

Exercise: My Personal Lifestyle

Complete the following sentences as though your life were exactly as you would like it to be. Let this be an accurate reflection of what you envision for your **ideal** life. After you have completed all these pieces of your Personal Vision, you can write a summary paragraph that encapsulates all your intentions, desires, and values.

1. In my family life I am committed to _____
_____ (spending time with, enjoying, teaching, working with, taking care of) my spouse, partner, friends, family, and/or children).

2. For recreation and fun, I enjoy
_____
_____.

3. My home environment will be
_____
_____.

(nurturing, comfortable, a place for entertainment, on the water, spacious, have a home office, in the city, in the country, etc.)

4. My retirement home will be

_____

_____.

(a cabin in the mountains, a seaside condo, a small restored Victorian home, a large, spacious home to accommodate visiting grandchildren and guests, a large motor home, a houseboat, etc.)

5. My hobbies, passions, interest are

_____

_____.

(world travel, politics, reading, writing, sports, gardening, martial arts, etc.)

6. I will maintain (or regain) my health by

_____

_____.

(exercising, eating healthy foods, lowering my stress, meditating, etc.)

Exercise: My Professional Life
1. I will concentrate my practice in the areas of

_____

_____.

(fill in with niche or types of clients)

2. My office environment will be

_____

_____.

(spacious, comfortable, a home office, efficient, well-organized, etc.)

3. My financial plans are to

_____

_____.

(earn a minimum of _____ per year, save 20% of my income, leverage my investments to retire at age_____ with a yearly income of _____, allow for 4 vacations a year, buy a retirement home, etc.)

4. My business philosophy is one of

_____

_____ .

(integrity, leadership, dedication to my clients, providing superior coaching and modeling for my clients, being known as an expert in my specialty, etc.)

Personal Vision Worksheet
Using the information you have gathered about yourself in the preceding exercises, write your Personal Vision in paragraph from. You may do a rough draft and then polish it in the weeks to come.

In my personal life I am committed to

_____

_____ .

In my professional life I am committed to

_____

_____ .

This exercise was adapted from Shawn McNalis with Atticus of Orlando, and used with permission.

GOALS

What goals, aspirations, desires, intentions do you want to accomplish in the first six months of life coaching?

Business:

Personal:

What do you want to accomplish, change, or create in the first 30 days of life coaching?

Business:

Personal:

What I hope to gain from this coaching relationship:

Other things I'd like my coach to know about me:

SESSION PREPARATION FORM

Date: _____

To get the most out of your coaching session it is best to spend several minutes preparing for it. Please e-mail or fax me a copy before your session.

What I have accomplished since our last session: my wins or victories

☐

☐

☐

What I didn;t get done, but want to be held accountable for

☐

☐

☐

Challenges I am facing right now

☐

☐

☐

What I am appreciative of or grateful/thankful for?

☐

☐

☐

How do I want to use my coach today and what do I want to get out of this call?

☐

☐

☐

What I commit to doing before the next session.

☐

☐

☐

References

Adler, A. (1998). *Understanding human nature.* (C. Brett, Trans.). Center City, MN: Hazelden.

Adler, A. (1956). *The individual psychology of Alfred Adler: A systematic presentation in selections from his writings.* (H. L. Ansbacher & R. R. Ansbacher, Eds.). New York: Basic.

Albee, G. W. (1998). Fifty years of clinical psychology: Selling our soul to the devil. *Applied and Preventive Psychology, 7,* 189–194.

Albee, G. W. (2000, February). The Boulder model's fatal flaw. *American Psychologist, 55*(2), 247–248.

Allport, G. (1937). *Personality: A psychological interpretation.* New York: Holt.

Allport, G. (1955). *Becoming: Basic considerations for a psychology of personality.* New Haven, CT: Yale University Press.

Allport, G. (1961). *Pattern and growth in personality.* New York: Holt, Rinehart & Winston.

Assagioli, R. (1965). *Psychosynthesis: A manual of principles and techniques.* New York: Hobbs, Dorman.

Bandler, R., & Grindler, J. (1975). *Patterns of the hypnotic techniques of Milton H. Erickson, M.D.* Cupertino, CA: Meta.

Barlow, C. (1998). *Coaching toward excellence: Families and groups.* San Diego: The Quest Group.

Berg, I. K. (1994). *Family-based services: A solution-focused approach.* New York: Norton.

Bugental, J. F. T. (1967). *Challenges of humanistic psychology.* New York: McGraw-Hill.

Cameron, J. (1992). *The artist's way: A spiritual path to higher creativity.* Los Angeles, CA: Tarcher/Putnam.

Canfield, J., & Hansen, M.V. (1993). *Chicken soup for the soul: 101 stories to open the heart and rekindle the spirit.* Deerfield Beach, FL: Health Communications.

Capner, M., & Caltabiano, M. L. (1993). Factors affecting the progression towards burnout: A comparison of professional and volunteer counselors. *Psychological Reports, 73,* 555–561.

Davis, D., & Humphrey, K. (2000). *College counseling: Issues and strategies for the new millennium.* Alexandria, VA: American Counseling Association.

de Shazer, S. (1985). *Keys to solution in brief therapy.* New York: Norton.

de Shazer, S. (1988). *Clues: Investigating solutions in brief therapy.* New York: Norton.

Drucker, P. F. (1974). *Management: Tasks, responsibilities, practices.* New York: Harper & Row.

Ellis, D. (1998). *Life coaching: A new career for helping professionals.* Rapid City, SD: Breakthrough Enterprises.

Ellis, D. (1999). *Becoming a master student.* Boston: Houghton Mifflin.

Ellis, D. (2000). *Falling awake.* Rapid City, SD: Breakthrough Enterprises.

Ellis, D., & Lankowitz, S. (1995). *Human being.* Rapid City, SD: Breakthrough Enterprises.

Erickson, M. H. (1990). *Uncommon casebook: The complete clinical work of Milton H. Erickson.* (W. H. O'Hanlon & A. L. Hexum, Eds.). New York: Norton.

Fadiman, J., & Frager, R. (1976). *Personality and personal growth.* Upper Saddle River, NJ: Harper & Row.

Farber, B. A. (1990). Burnout in psychotherapists: Incidents, types and trends. *Psychotherapy in Private Practice, 8,* 35–44.

Feld, J. (1998). *SoHo Success Letter™.* E-mail: Judy@CoachNet.com. Web site: www.coachnet.com. Phone: 972-931-6366.

Figley, C. R. (1993). Compassion stress: Toward its measurement and management. *Family Therapy News,* issue 24.

Fortgang, L. B. (1998). *Take yourself to the top: The secrets of America's #1 career coach.* New York: Warner.

Frankl, V. E. (1959). *Man's search for meaning.* New York: Pocket.

Freud, S. (1965). *New introductory lectures on psychoanalysis.* New York: Norton.

Freud, S. (1982). *Basic works of Sigmund Freud.* (J. Strackey, Trans./Ed.). Franklin Center, PA: Franklin Library.

Freudenberger, H. J. (1974). Staff burnout. *Journal of Social Issues, 30*(1), 159–165.

Gilliland, B. E., & James, R. K. (1997). *Crisis intervention strategies.* Pacific Grove: Brooks/Cole.

Goble, F. (1971). *The third force: The psychology of Abraham Maslow.* New York: Simon & Schuster.

Goldberg, M. C. (1998). *The art of the question: A guide to short-term question-centered therapy.* New York: Wiley.

Goldstein, K. (1963). *Human nature in the light of psychopathology.* New York, Schocken.

Gottman, J. M. (1976). *A couple's guide to communication.* Champaign, IL: Research Press.

Gottman, J. (1999). *The seven principles for making marriage work.* New York: Crown.

Gottman, J. M., & DeClaire, J. (2001). *The relationship cure: A five-step guide for building better connections with family, friends, and lovers.* New York: Crown.

Gottman, J. M., & Silver, N. (1994). *The seven principles for making marriage work.* New York: Crown.

Haley, J. (1986). *Uncommon therapy: The psychiatric techniques of Milton H. Erickson.* New York: Norton.

Hargrove, R. (1995). *Masterful coaching.* San Diego: Pfeiffer.

Hayden, C. J. (1999). *Get clients now!: A 28-day marketing program for professionals and consultants.* New York: AMACOM.

Hendrix, H. (1988). *Getting the love you want: A guide for couples.* New York: Holt.

Hill, N. (1990). *Think and grow rich.* Los Angeles: Fawcett.

Horney, K. (1980). *The adolescent diaries of Karen Horney.* New York: Basic.

Hudson, F. (1999). *The handbook of coaching: A comprehensive resource guide for managers, executives, consultants, and HR.* San Francisco: Jossey-Bass.

Hudson, F. (1999). *The adult years.* San Francisco: Jossey-Bass.

Ivey, A. E. (1994). *Intentional interviewing and counseling: Facilitating client development in a multicultural society.* Pacific Grove, CA: Brooks.

Jourard, S. M. (1974). *Healthy personality, an approach from the viewpoint of humanistic psychology.* New York: Macmillan.

Jung, C. G. (1933). *Modern man in search of a soul.* London: Trubner.

Jung, C. G. (1953). *The collected works of C. G. Jung.* (H. Read, M. Fordham, & G. Adler, Eds.). New York: Pantheon.

Jung, C. G. (1970). *Civilization in transition.* (R. F. C. Hull, Trans.). Princeton, NJ: Princeton University Press.

Jung, C. G. (1976). *The portable Jung.* (J. Campbell, Ed.; R. F. C. Hull, Trans.). New York: Penguin.

Kesey, K. (1962). *One flew over the cuckoo's nest, a novel.* New York: Viking.

Klein, H. (2000, October). Practice building: The coaching phenomenon marches on. *Psychotherapy Finances, 26*(7), 5–7.

Lecky, P. (1945). *Self-consistency: A theory of personality.* New York: Island Press.

Leonard, T. (1998). *The portable coach.* New York: Scribner.

Lewin, K. (1935). *A dynamic theory of personality.* New York: McGraw-Hill.

Lewin, K. (1938). *The conceptual representation and the measurement of psychological forces.* Durham, NC: Duke University Press.

Lowry, S., & Menendez, D. (1997). *Discovering your best self through the art of coaching.* Houston: NexusPoint/Enterprise.

Madanes, C. (1981). *Strategic family therapy.* San Francisco: Jossey-Bass.

Madanes, C. (1984). *Behind the one-way mirror: Advances in the practice of strategic therapy.* San Francisco: Jossey-Bass.

Maslach, C. (1982). *Burnout: The cost of caring.* Englewood Cliffs, NJ: Prentice-Hall.

Maslow, A. (1954). *Motivation and personality.* New York: Harper.

Maslow, A. (1962). *Toward a psychology of being.* Princeton, NJ: Van Nostrand.

Maslow, A. (1993). *Farther reaches of human nature.* New York: Arkana.

May, R. (1953). *Man's search for himself.* New York: Norton.

May, R. (1975). *The courage to create.* New York: Norton.

May, R. (1979). *Psychology and the human dilemma.* New York: Norton.

McGraw, P. (1999). *Life strategies: Doing what works, doing what matters.* New York: Hyperion.

Myers, J. E. (1991). Wellness as the paradigm for counseling and development: The possible future. *Counselor Education and Supervision, 30,* 183–193.

O'Hanlon, B. (1999a). *Guide to possibility land.* New York: Norton.

O'Hanlon, B. (1999b). *Do one thing different.* New York: Morrow.

O'Hanlon, W. H., & Martin, M. (1992). *Solution-oriented hypnosis: An Ericksonian approach.* New York: Norton.

Perls, F. S. (1966). *Ego, hunger and aggression: A revision of Freud's theory and method.* San Francisco: Orbit Graphics Arts.

Perls, F. S. (1973). *The Gestalt approach and eye witness to therapy.* Ben Lomand, CA: Science & Behavior.

Phillips, B. (1999). *Body for life.* New York: HarperCollins.

Prather, H. (1970). *Notes to myself.* Moab, Utah: Real People Press.

Richardson, C. (1998). *Take time for your life: A personal coach's seven step program for creating the life you want.* New York: Broadway.

Richardson, C. (2000). *Life makeovers.* New York: Broadway.

Ries, L., & Ries, A. (1998). *The 22 immutable laws of branding.* New York: HarperBusiness.

Rilke, R. M. (1904). *Letters to a young poet.* (M. D. Herter, Trans.). New York: Norton.

Rogers, C. (1951). *Client-centered therapy.* Boston: Houghton Mifflin.

Satir, V. (1964). *Conjoint family therapy: A guide to therapy and techniques.* Palo Alto, CA: Science & Behavior.

Satir, V. (1976). *Making contact.* Millbrae, CA: Celestial Arts.

Satir, V. (1991). *Satir model: Family therapy & beyond.* Palo Alto: Science & Behavior.

Satir, V., & Baldiwin, M. (1983). *Step by step: A guide to creating change in families.* Palo Alto, CA: Science & Behavior.

Schaufeli, W. B., Maslach, C., & Marek, T. (Eds.). (1993). *Professional burnout: Recent developments in theory and research.* Washington, DC: Taylor & Francis.

Schneider, K. J., Bugental, J. F. T., Pierson, J. F. (Eds.). (2002). *The handbook of humanistic psychology.* Thousand Oaks, CA: Sage.

Steele, D. (1997). Professional coaching and the marriage and family therapist. *California Therapist, 12*(2), 54–55.

Toffler, A. (1970). *Future shock.* New York: Bantam.

Walter, J., & Peller, J. (2000). *Recreating brief therapy: Preferences and possibilities.* New York: Norton.

Weiner-Davis, M. (1992). *Divorce busting: A revolutionary and rapid program for staying together.* New York: Summit.

Whitmore, J. (1995). *Coaching for performance.* Sonoma, CA: Nicholas Brealey.

Whitworth, L., Kimsey-House, H., & Sandahl, P. (1998). *Co-active coaching*. Palo Alto, CA: Davies-Black.

Williams, P. (1980). *Transpersonal psychology: An introductory guidebook*. Greeley, CO: Lutey.

Williams, P. (1997). Telephone coaching for cash draws new client market. *Practice Strategies, 2*, 11.

Williams, P. (1999). The therapist as personal coach: Reclaiming your soul! *The Independent Practitioner, 19*(4), 204–207.

Williams, P. (2000a, July). Practice building: The coaching phenomenon marches on. *Psychotherapy Finances, 26*(315), 1–2.

Williams, P. (2000b, June). Personal coaching's evolution from therapy, *Consulting Today* [Special issue], 4.

Zieg, J. K. (1994). *Ericksonian methods: The essence of the story*. New York: Brunner/Mazel.

Index

About the Authors

Patrick Williams, Ed.D., MCC, is a "recovered" psychologist and life coach, author, speaker, and trainer with over 20 years experience in the arena of personal excellence. He is a licensed clinical psychologist but has always been nontraditional in his training and approach to effective living. Pat received his bachelor's degree from Kansas University, and a master's degree in humanistic psychology from West Georgia College, and completed his doctorate in transpersonal psychology from the University of Northern Colorado. Pat has written several articles on coaching as well as chapters for other books. This is his first book about life coaching.

The joyfulness of coaching people to "design a life, not just get over a past" moved him into full-time coaching in 1995 after having a psychotherapy practice for 16 years. Pat likes to say, "I used to be a *shrink* . . . now I am an *enlarger!*" In 1996, Pat closed his psychology practice after building up a coaching clientele and moved to Florida for 3 years, working exclusively by telephone with international clients. He trained and graduated from Coach University in 1997, and within that same year the International Coach Federation designated him a Master Certified Coach. In 1998, he saw the need for a specialized coach-training program for mental health professionals and founded Therapist University, which is now called the Institute for Life Coach Training. Since 1998, it has trained hundreds of therapists and counselors to add life coaching to their businesses.

Pat and his wife, Jill, now live in the countryside near Ft. Collins, Colorado, where his heart sings and they both delight in the variety and awesomeness of nature.

In all of his professional endeavors, Pat brings a whole-person approach to his work and conducts his life with integrity, a deep sense of caring, and a lightness of spirit. His mission is to impact profoundly the lives of those he coaches and trains so that they may profoundly impact the lives of others.

Deborah C. Davis, Ed. D., NCC, ACS, LMFT, is a certified life coach (CLC) and author with more than 26 years of experience in the human effectiveness field. She is a licensed family therapist and retired university professor emeritus with specialities in counseling and adult education.

Deb did her undergraduate and graduate work at Albertson's College in Idaho and earned a doctorate in human resource development from Boston University. Not only is she a masterful life coach with a thriving practice, she also teaches graduate level courses, presents frequently at national conferences, and is recognized as an outstanding mentor and motivational speaker. She is the CEO of Human Dynamics, a human potential institute, where she collaborates with individuals who want to optimize their personal performances and create their lives in different, more meaningful ways.

On a personal note, Deb is married to Dennis Edwards, her wonderful life partner and best friend. They have four adult children and two grandchildren. Deb and Dennis actively cocreate the lives of their dreams, which they envision as spending summers working on their ranch in the mountains of Idaho and winters relaxing on the beaches of Maui.

Deb works diligently to help her clients discover what is deeply important to them and then nurtures their efforts toward what really matters most. Deb loves to laugh and brings humor and love into her work and life on a daily basis.